When I was Lifted Up

The Master Candle

From an Orphan to Standing in Front of the Lord

THE BEGINNING

William Holsclaw

ISBN 978-1-64559-984-5 (Paperback)
ISBN 978-1-63814-071-9 (Hardcover)
ISBN 978-1-64559-985-2 (Digital)

Covenant Books, Inc.
11661 Hwy 707
Murrells Inlet, SC 29576
www.covenantbooks.com

Down from the
tree He came
Looking for me
and you!

THE TITLE OF THE BOOK IS [WHEN I WAS LIFTED UP]

These are the people who helped make my book come to life.

Melanie M. Holsclaw
Joe Holsclaw
Robert and Betty Stevens
Elaine and Jerry Young
Mr. and Mrs. S. Baughman
Felicia M. Shoemaker
Nancy Pearson
Joel L. Kathy Denniston
Doris A. Twitty
Bill and Linda Graves
Jean Ruse
Tamra J. Randolph
Paige Werner
Becky S. Robbins
Robert M. and Jenni Sprague
Daniel E. Love
Bruce and Sherry Wessel
Rev. Tarrence Chatman
Irvin and Marsha A. Hosfield
Karen and Jerry Twitty
Lynn D. and Jean M. Sheets
Warrens Lawn, LANDSCAPE Inc.
Barb Denniston

I am the master candle

Contents

People in My life/Writings..1

In My life 2

All life 2

Winds 2

Heart's door 3

Because 4

Back 4

Spirit 4

Who Is Greater Than You? 4

The Candle 6

As I Walk through Life 7

Flower 8

Some of the Things That Happened to Me 9

This Is the Story of William W. Holsclaw 12

Life in the Cary Home 29

School Days 34

Joe Over the Hill 35

Big Boys in Charge 37

Making an Old Bike 40

Making Fun of My Old Bike 42

The Night the Electricity Went Out 44

Cary Home Highlights 47

Jerry and the Sled 49

Dinosaur in the Woods 52

Under Attack at My Fort 54

The Wrong Family for Me 57

New Bike 59

Joe and the Gum 61

Mortuary Business 62

Visiting the Avenue 65

Last Day in the Cary Home 66

Moving On 71

Working at TV Clinic 75

Seeing Lynn 77

Reading the Bible 80

Does God See You? 84

Hunting out West 87

Our Old New House 89

In a Roman Village 90

Walking with Jesus 91

Tina Calls for Help 92

Cell Phone from God 93

Golden Gloves of Trustworthiness 94

Lampstand 96

Truck Stuck in the Snow 97

A Lot of Money in My Hands 100

Ball Silicon Stretchy String 101

Tennis Dream 104

Helping Our Pastor's Wife 106

Job in Detroit, Michigan 107

Waiting for My Help 110

Little Old Man 112

Ten Dolls 114

Talking to Pastor Daniel 116

UFOs 117

If Only I Had a Stick 118

Working in Chicago 121

When I Was Lifted Up 125

The Lord's Joy and Love 130

Seeing the Mother of Christ 131

Telling God's Children What He Did for Me 133

Nativity Scene 136

The Night I Saw My Soul 138

Path 142

Precognition 145

How Did This Man Know Who I Was 146

Real Time That Is Different 147

I - 65 South 148

Golden Gates of Heaven 149

People in My life/Writings

This book would not be possible if it wasn't for friends in my life and family.

I would like to thank them now. My sister Marquita, who had pictures of the Cary Home and a newspaper clipping of the people who donated money to have the building built on Eighteenth Street, in Lafayette, Indiana. Jessie Levering Cary donated money to build and open the home for children. The home opened in the year of November 30, 1930.

Some of the old pictures are of the children and Marquita's girlfriends, who lived there at the time she was living there. Some old automobiles used to haul kids to school when the weather was bad and in the wintertime.

I would like to thank my wife, Melanie, for helping me to write the book and a pamphlet two years after I was lifted up, when I stood in front of the Lord. I now pass the pamphlet out to people that I come across in my life. I was told by the Lord to tell his children what he did for me.

And now I am lifting the Lord up and writing a book of what He did in my life to get the word out to more Christians and help them to be lifted up by His love. For them to know that the way the Lord worked in my time of need, the Lord will work in the same way in your time of need also. He is here waiting for us all.

I prayed to the Lord that He would send someone to help me with the editing of the book, not knowing that the person would be one of the teachers that work with the children in the Sunday school classes in the First Church of God in Frankfort, Indiana.

When you purchase one of the books, you will be helping with the mission fields. All the proceeds from selling the books will go to the funding of the missions to help people we don't know in other parts of the country and the world. They need all the help they can get, and thanks to you for all your support.

I would like to thank Jenni S. for helping me with the editing of the book. Without her help, it would have been months before I could have sent it to the publisher to see if it would be accepted for printing.

And big thanks to God and the Lord, who does hear me and helped me to complete my book.

IN MY LIFE FROM BIRTH
GOD AND THE LORD TO
THE END OF MY LIFE

ALL LIFE HAS A STARTING PLACE
THERE IS A BEGINNING AND THERE IS AN END

WHAT HAPPENS IN THE MIDDLE
DEPENDS ON WHAT HAPPENS IN THE END

WINDS

When the winds of time blow in the beginning of our lives, we don't know where they are going or where the winds are taking us. But we travel the road that the winds lead us on, from the first day of our lives to the last days of our lives.

Put God in your life. He is in charge of the winds.

HEART'S DOOR

WHO STANDS AT MY DOOR AND KNOCKS

A SOFT GENTLE KNOCK

ON MY HEART'S DOOR

I OPEN THE DOOR TO PEEK OUT

THERE THE LORD STANDS

GLOWING WITH LOVE FOR ME

HE HOLDS HIS HAND OUT

AND I TAKE IT, AND HE SAYS TO ME

THE ROAD IS HARD, BUT TOGETHER

WE CAN MAKE IT

I AM HERE FOR YOU, AND ALL MY CHILDREN

COME AND FOLLOW ME

Written By: William W. Holsclaw

Because

You are who you are because of who you were yesterday. And tomorrow you will be because of who you are today. It's best to think about what you do now so you can be with God: He who has loved you, the greatness, from the beginning of God's time.

Back

There is a love around the corner, that's called God
That you turned your back on
But God never turned His back on you

Spirit

With Your mighty hand, Your Spirit moves across this land, with a love that is the same for me as for you (the reader).

Who Is Greater Than You?

Who will stand in front of the storms of life for you? As God waters his flowers, God also waters your soul. When I cry out, "God help me," God sees me, God hears me, and God knows me, because God is the real love in the I AM.

THE GREAT TRUTH
TRUTH IS THE SAME TODAY AND TOMORROW
YOU CANNOT ADD TO IT
YOU CANNOT TAKE AWAY FROM IT
IT IS ALWAYS THE SAME
IT IS GOD

I had a dream that I was in the shower, and I looked down at my feet and I couldn't see the water. To see the water's edge, I would need to look at the side walls and the floor where the water would meet; it was hard to see the water because it was super clean and crystal clear.

Then out of nowhere, objects started falling into the crystal water. But it wouldn't mix with the water of truth. The water stayed clean, unmoved by the objects that it was being hit with, the waste of humanity, like lies, sin, and all the other iniquities and impurities.

This is what God is. I am what I am. I don't change, and you can't change me.

You have three choices in life to see God:

1. Love God with all your soul.
2. Love your neighbor with your whole soul.
3. Love yourself and treat it as a temple.

Then you will see the love that is waiting for you.

The Candle

There is a Candle that never burns out; it shows the way for all that turn to find its light.

We were all part of the Candle once, but our light burned out, left us in the darkness. Then sin moved in.

God was not able to light our candle. We lived in the world of no light, any light, just sin.

The Master Candle sent another Candle to light the way.

Then one day, when we felt lost, the need to turn to the Light, then the Light saw that we were looking for the Living Light.

The Lord did reach down and pull us out of the darkness, to light our candle, so we might know of His love that lights us on our walk back home to the Master Candle. What a joy!

As I Walk through Life

As I walk in life, the Lord talks to me

My heart jumps with joy
As I walk through my life
I know that I am being led by Him
Who has my best interest in His hands for me
I find Him standing at all my crossroads
Leading me by my hand in the right path.

Flower

There was a flower that lived in the desert of sin. It had all the things this world could give it: friends, family, money, and health. Then other flowers came by to talk about the good life. Then the rain of life came by to give it the drops of the living water of love and life, and to feed it the everlasting bread of life and light its candle to shine in the world of darkness.

But the flower said it didn't need any of it as it was very happy with what it had, and it said, "No, thanks!" So the water of life moved on, never, it seemed, to come by again.

Over time, the flower started to wilt, but it was too late to ask for water. It was drying up! The good times were gone, health, money, and friends. Now it had lost all the joy, love, and hope. These were always there, but had been covered up by its sins. Now it was having the lonely life, and what it missed most was love.

But the Lord of love had kept an eye on the flower, and saw that it had put its faith in the world. So the Lord of life gave the flower a drop of living water, and it came back to life. This is what true love is. That the Lord of love has for every flower in the world.

The moral of the story is God doesn't give up on us. We are always on His mind. We are His beautiful flower forever!

Some of the Things That Happened to Me

Because of all the different things that happened to me in my life, most people will find it hard to believe that this many things could happen to one person.

When this took place, it happened in real time, driving my truck to work. I was lifted up and out of my body, and my soul saw the Lord in his glory. Then I was given the privilege of not only seeing the Lord, but He flooded my soul with His overwhelming love. I was standing next to an angel in a brown robe, and at the same time my soul was standing on seven steps.

Some of the other things that happened in my life were when an angel made a brick wall disappear, then He was standing in the open wall, looking down at me and my soul. Later in my life I realized this was the same angel that was standing next to me, on the seven steps when I saw the Lord in His glory.

When I received a telephone call from my niece, a question was asked me. The next thing I knew, I was looking down into a well, through my mind's eye, seeing a bubble coming up from the bottom. As it came to the top, it burst at the surface, and gave me the answer to the question.

In another dream I was able to see what the weather would be in two weeks, and see myself with a lot of money in my hands. This shirt had two front pockets on the front of it, with money hanging out of them! So much money that some fell to the ground!

These are some of the things that happened to me, in my journey through my life. Some occurred in real time, others in dreams, which were very vivid. Their memories stay with me like they just happened.

It was a very hot summer day: Dick loaded us up in the old Ford truck to go swimming out at the Wild Cat Creek. I almost lost my life on that day. It feels like it just happened yesterday.

Sometimes, in prayer, when I needed help, or when I was in trouble, I called upon the Lord. Just like when my truck was stuck in the snow. He heard me and helped me.

I would see things that I didn't ask for and wonder why, like new worlds, where you didn't walk.

I was sixteen when a friend of mine who went to Jefferson High School called to see if I would like a summer job after school was out.

I said, "Sure, but I will need to talk to Larry at the Cary Home to see if it was OK with him." I did get the job, doing the pans at the restaurant in Mar-Jean Mall on South Street.

After I got off work at 10:00 p.m., I had to walk home. I turned off south Eighteenth Street, and there was no lighting as I was walking down the driveway.

When I came to were the road would take you to the back of the Cary Home, as I was heading to the right, someone called my name:

"Bill!" It was a woman's voice that was soft and sweet sounding. It came from above me, but as I looked up at the windows, where the older girls' dorm was, I didn't see any girls looking out of the windows. There was no one.

I turned and started walking again, and I heard the voice call my name again, "Bill!" I was gone as fast as I could run to the back of the building and in the door. I thought to myself, some of the girls would be making fun of me in the morning, but no one said anything to me.

I did wonder who it was that called my name that night. Fifty-two years later I would find out who it was that called my name.

There are many more things that opened my eyes, and my ears. As you read the book, you'll find many more unusual events that will make you wonder. I hope that by reading about my experiences, you will know that you are not alone! God and the Lord's love are there for all to find.

Back Row: left to right
Harold Guy "Sonny" Richardson (half brother)
Gordon Leroy "Buster" Holsclaw

Second Row: left to right
Richard Eugene "Dick" Holsclaw
Marquita May Holsclaw holding
baby Hazel Annette Holsclaw

Third Row: left to right
Joseph Allen "Joe" Holsclaw
James Leroy "Jim" Holsclaw

Fourth Row: left to right
William Willard "Bill" Holsclaw
Lynn Dewayne "Lynn" Holsclaw

This Is the Story of William W. Holsclaw

I was born on August 4, 1941, in the town of Lafayette, Indiana. I lived in a family that had eight children. I was number seven. There would be a total of nine in the family. We lived in the north end of the town on Eighteenth Street, a poor blue-collar neighborhood.

My first remembrance was that I was standing outside in the summertime, looking across the street at the house that was on fire, and the firemen were trying to put it out. It was put out and under control, and life went back to normal.

When Mom wanted my dad, she would send us three boys down to the corner tavern that was a half block from our house, to get him to come home to eat. We would look into the tavern to see if he was there, and the bar tender would see us peeking in the window of the front door. He would yell, "Roy, your kids are here!" You could see that he was not happy with us when he got up from the back of the room and headed our way. He was like a redheaded bull. We knew it was time to run. The smoke was coming out of his nostrils from his cigarette; we would try not to laugh too hard! We ran as fast as we could to get back home, with him chasing after us. Just as we were sitting down at the table, he would burst into the house and sat down not saying a word, shoveling the food into his mouth as fast as he could. Unlike most fathers who would read the newspaper after supper, he never did. Every evening he would go back to the tavern to finish playing cards.

On the corner of Eighteenth and Schuyler Avenue, there were three taverns and a drug store, and one block south of Schuyler Avenue on the west side stood a grocery store. If you were lucky, you could catch the bread man delivering bread to the-grocery store. He would pass out little loaves of bread to the kids that were hanging around, who were anxiously waiting for him to show up in his bread truck.

When I was five years old, we moved to Mc Dowel Avenue and Moore Street. I think Dad moved us to keep us from coming to the tavern and getting him to come home to eat. He really wanted to play cards and drink. We moved to a house that had six rooms, but by that time there was one more child in the family, a baby girl named Hazel.

Here is the layout of the exterior of our new house: looking from the front of the house, standing in the street that was made of gravel, you first would see a row of hedges in front with an opening in the middle. It was open so that you could walk up a path of dirt to the front porch. We lived in a poor neighborhood, thanks to my dad, and his bad habits.

This house had five rooms in it and a back porch, not heated, with an outhouse in the far corner of the back yard. When you would go in the front door, you would be standing in the living room. There was a telephone sitting on a stand. Next to it is a very large couch that would turn into a bed at night. My brother Joe and Bill would sleep at one end, then the other end my sister Mark and my brother Lynn. In the far corner of the room was where the potbellied stove sat, there was a door to the right. That went into the kitchen. In the center of the living room ceiling, was one light hanging on the AC wire, with a socket for the bulb and a switch with a pull chain to turn the light on or off.

To your left, next to the wall, was a full size standing radio, where we would sit around on the floor and listen to baseball games, and shows like *The Shadow* and more stories, then the news. There were just bare floors, throughout the house, in the exits and entrances of the doors were throw rugs made by hand out of rags. The door next to the radio was a bedroom where Mom and Dad and baby Hazel would sleep. To the right of Dad's door was another bedroom where Sonny, Buster, Dick, and Jim would sleep.

When you walked into the kitchen, to your left, was a stove that would burn wood. You could cook on the other half with bottled gas. To the right of the stove was a sink, with only cold water. The room next to the kitchen was a dining room with a big round table and chairs. The last room was the back room and a door that we would keep shut in the wintertime, because it was unheated in the wintertime. In that room we would store the wringer washer, a rinse bucket, and the chair with no back on it that we used to sit the tub on to do the laundry in the kitchen.

There was a big apricot tree standing in the front yard, to the left of the dirt path. I would climb it to find out if the apricots were good to eat, but first you would open them up and look for worms. I spent many hours up in the tree when the fruit was ready to eat.

To the right corner of the yard, up front was an old garage. Next to us was an old house. That belonged to an old man we called "Jack the Bootlegger." On Sundays he would sell whiskey to his customers, whoever would come around. That was his way to subsidize his income; he didn't have a wife or children that I ever saw.

There were only four homes on our block, facing our house and to the right was Jack's house. To the left of our house was a woman that I never remember ever seeing. Someone live there, because the lights would be on at night. In the last house next to Monon train yards, lived a women and her husband. The kids called her the "Candy Lady."

At the far corner of the yard, there stood an old outhouse that was our outdoor bathroom. The outhouse was a one-seater, like most bathrooms, in the house or outside. When you really had to go bad, there was always someone already in there, and they had the door locked! You could look through the crack in the door and yell at him, that you had to go really bad, as you jumped up and down holding on to the thing that had to go. Then they might open the door, see who was out there. One time it was Joe. He would take his sweet old time. "Hurry up, I got to go bad!" I yelled. I looked around for a stick to put it in the crack. I lifted up on the wood door lock, and the door would swing open wide by itself, and Joe would come out pulling up his pants. The good part about following someone in the outhouse in the summertime was that all the flies would be gone. If you were first in the summertime, when you would sit down, all the flies and bees would fly between your legs, trying to get out. Maybe that's how the people who cleaned out outhouses got their name honey dippers!

There was a chicken coop just over our hill in the back yard, with New York Bandy chickens, which we were trying to raise for their eggs. When you'd try to get the eggs, they would fly in your face, but Dad didn't like that, so he got rid of them for good. So from that time on, to get eggs, Joe, Jim, Lynn, and I would go next door to Bootlegger Jack. We would crawl under his chicken coop that was behind his house, just over the hill. Just like in our chicken coop, the hens would lay their eggs under the hen house, where no one could reach them.

Only a very small person could get to their nest at the very top, where the building and the dirt came together. That person was our youngest brother, Lynn. He would get all of them, and we would take them to Mom to cook up for us to eat. If we didn't get the eggs they would spoil and become known as rotten eggs.

When we would go to the duck pond, we would go over the hill and cross over State Road 52 north, and down over another hill to the pond. Here we would catch fish, frogs, and snakes.

My dad was a true redhead, and his nickname was Red. He worked on the Monon railroad, which was only half a block from our house. I don't know what my mother ever saw in him, I only know him as being old to me, and never being home. When he was home, he was usually drunk, and fighting with my mother. If it wasn't for my older brother Sonny, who would step in between them and break them up and stop the fight, Mom would have been the loser. She was a thin, black-haired woman about five feet and five inches tall. Unfortunately for us kids, my father liked living in the bars and not being home. That's why we didn't see him very much. In the long run, it turned out to be good for my mother. My mother was a very hard worker. Every night she would wash us down so we would be clean when we went to bed. We had no hot water, and it had to be heated on the kitchen stove, every night, seven days a week. We would take turns getting our bath. It was always colder in the wintertime when it came to taking a bath. The way we would run around, we would get holes in our pant knees, and she would sit down in the evening and would patch the holes in our worn out pants. In the long run, she was very good to us.

To wash our clothes, she had an old wringer washer with a rinse tub set up in the kitchen, and used a wooden stick to get the clothes out of the tub. In the summertime she could hang the clothes outside on the clothesline to dry. When winter would come, she would put up a clothesline that stretched all over the kitchen to dry the wet clothes inside the house.

It was cold in the kitchen. Our sink would freeze up, and the water could not run out of the pipe. There was a long stick outside that we used to break the ice up in the drain, and then the water would flow out and down the hill.

When winter came, it would get very cold. It would get so cold in the house that if any water was left in the basin, it would freeze up by morning. Most houses had no insulation in the walls, so when the wind would blow, you could feel the cold air coming through the windows.

Before we would get up to get dressed, we would wait for someone to start a fire in the potbellied stove in the living room, or the kitchen stove, the part that used bottle gas to cook. Then we jumped out of bed and took our clothes with us. Once when I tried to put my shoes on, I had something inside at the toe of my shoe, so I gave it to one of my older brothers. (I had seen a wiggling tail.) He reached inside and pulled out a mouse! He opened up the door of the old potbellied stove and threw it inside and burned it up.

When we went to play outside we would put on our navy coats; they were very heavy and warm, with big buttons on them, with an anchor imprint on face of the buttons.

Some days my dad would have some men over from work to play cards and drink beer around our round oak dining room table. We would hang around the table like hawks looking at their cards. Sometimes they would give us money to get us out of their hair. Then we would head for the drug store to buy candy for everyone.

Joe would buy a pack of cigarettes for him, not candy, but Jim and I would get candy, a Baby Ruth. Now with a pack of cigarettes, Joe wouldn't be walking in the gutters looking for cigarette butts, that were still lit, and he would smoke them. You might wonder why he didn't steal Dad's cigarettes, but if you had watched dad roll a cigarette, you'd understand: The first thing he would do was to take out the paper, and hold it between his two index fingers, then he'd pour out the tobacco into the paper. Next he'd take his tongue and lick it from one end to the other. It would be all wet, and it looked awful!

In the wintertime, we would help cut kindling for the potbellied stove and the kitchen stove. Half of the kitchen stove was wood burning, and the other half was bottled gas. Kindling was the only way Mom could get the coal to start burning. The potbellied stove sat in the corner of the living room. There was no furnace in the basement. The only thing in the basement was the coal bin. I would carry up the coal in a coal bucket. It was the same bucket that I used to carry out the ashes from the stove, and dump them over the hill. Sometimes I dumped the ashes on the snow to walk on in the wintertime to the outhouse, or in the driveway so the car wouldn't get stuck in the snow.

The house was too small for a family of nine and two parents.

The sleeping order was my mother, father, and baby Hazel in the front bedroom. In the other bedroom, my brothers Sonny, Gordon (Buster), Richard (Dick), and Jim. On one end of the couch, Lynn and my sister Marquita (Mark), and on the other end was Joe and myself (Bill). The problem with Joe was he wet the bed, and during the night, I would feel it coming my way and try to get out of the way.

Sometimes Jim, Joe, and I would go over to the railroad yards and crawl under the fence. We would go to the far end of the tracks, and we would get one of the work carts that were on the tracks and shove the cart down the tracks. We would ride it for a good two blocks, and ride it into the barricade (dead man) at the end, where the tracks would come to a dead end. We would jump off before it hit the dead end, watch the cart fly through the air. Behind us we would hear detective Bowman yelling as he came running out of the work shed ordering us to stop, or he was going to call the police on us. He was overweight, and by then we were hitting the ground, running and laughing. By the time we were crawling under the fence, we were only half a block from our home. We would hide behind the hedges and watch for the cops, but they never did come by.

Sometimes when we were in the railroad yards we would find coal, and coal that was used up north in the steel mills to make the fires burn very hot, to help melt the steel. We would take whatever fell off the rail cars and take it home to our house and use it in our potbellied stove, which helped to heat our home in the wintertime. My father made good money working on the railroad, and could have bought fuel to heat the house, if only he could stay out of the taverns, and stop spending his money on drinking, and playing cards, and cigarettes.

By this time, we had nine children in the family, and this is their order of birth: Sonny, Gordon, Dick, Marquita, Jim, Joe, William, Lynn, and the very last one were a girl, named Hazel. I had six brothers and two sisters. I was the seventh in the family.

I am now writing this book at the age of seventy-six years old. Out of nine brothers and sisters, there are five of us left: Gordon, Marquita, Joe, Bill, and Lynn. The ones that have passed on are Sonny, Dick, Jim, and Hazel. At this time it seems only right to mention their names.

There are many things that happened to me as I was growing up. At the beginning, some of them where spiritual, some were dreams, and some were in real time. What I mean by "real time" is that I was awake and aware of what was going on. Some people call it a vision.

One of the things that happened to me when I was four years old was my older brother Dick said that he would take us swimming with him and his friend at the Wildcat Creek. So we all jumped into the back of the truck: Jim, Joe, and Bill. Then we held on, as we went down the winding, gravel road, until we ended up far into the country, where we would get to the best swimming hole.

When we pulled into the road that took us to the creek, the old Ford truck came to a stop. We all jumped out and ran down to the sandbar. My brothers Jim and Joe jumped into the water; I played on the sandbar, because I didn't know how to swim nor trusted the water. Dick's friend reached down and picked me up and threw me into the creek and said, "I'll show you how to get him to swim!"

As soon as I hit the water, I was looking at pictures of my family as they flashed before my eyes. It was as though I was looking at the pictures with a lampshade on my head, and as it turned, it would stop and I would see a picture of my dad, and then it would spin fast and stop, then I would see a picture of my mom, and so on. The next thing I knew I was lying on a sandbar coughing up in the water that was in my lungs. Then my brother Dick said it was time to go home.

So we all climbed back into the truck. As we were going down the gravel road, I noticed that my brother Dick and his friend, who was up in front, driving the truck, were passing a bottle of whiskey back and forth and laughing.

As we were coming to the first turn in the road, I said to my brother Joe that the truck was going to go over the hill on the next turn. As we came to the next turn of the road, the truck went over the road and slid down the bank, the truck was stuck halfway down, on some trees. Everything in the truck bed went to the bottom of the hill; it was very hard to believe that none of us got hurt, except the truck.

If the tree was not there, the truck would of rolled on down the hill to the bottom, and the driver and my bother Dick could have gotten broken bones or worse, thrown out the windows and rolled over by the truck, and the ones sitting in the bed of the truck, would fly through the air and the truck could have of rolled over us, broken some of our bones, or killed us.

That was the first time that I was able to foresee the future, or an event before it happened. One of the things that I learned from this, even when I was drowning in the creek, and the truck going over the hill, was that there was Someone who was watching over me. We all crawled back up to the top of the road, and started walking home.

When I look back now, I see why God watches over His children. He shows us that He is a loving God. When you care, He cares and knows you are trying to find the right path to Him.

My sister Marquita and I would go to church at the Salvation Army. We would catch the city bus to go downtown and walk to church on north Fourth Street. My class was in the basement, and as I would sit in small chairs for little people, the teacher was telling me that I had a black heart, full of sin.

"I don't have a black heart!" I said.

Then Mark, my sister, came to get me to go upstairs to the church service in the main hall.

My sister sang in a volunteer group for WASK Radio Station downtown. I don't know how she got the job, but she was going to take Jim with her. He didn't want to go, neither did Joe, but I said I would. This was the first time I ever went to town and rode a city bus. As I sat in the studio, I was enjoying a Coke in my hand, and it was all mine. Another first in my life!

My brothers and I found a way to improve the neighborhood! We boys would throw rocks at the streetlight at night to see who could put it out. In a couple of days, the city would put another bulb in, but after two or three times, they put a wire cage around the bulb. However, we were able to throw stones through the cage, and it still went out. Then the city black-topped the road in front of our house, and the light never went out again! No rocks.

I had a friend who lived up the street that lived next to an old man. This old man would sit on his front porch, holding a rope around the neck of his goat. The goat's job was to eat the grass up. Day after day, when you'd walk by, you would see him sitting on the porch, and the goat doing his job.

My friend wasn't home so I turned around and headed back home. Standing in front of my house was my friend Mike. He had a candy bar that he was eating.

I said, "Where did you get that?"

He said, "From the candy lady on the corner. Do you want one? All you need to do is let her pull your pants down, and let her play with you." There were a lot of boys that would get a candy bar from her, but not me.

I told him, "That's not for me!"

The last thing I remember at the far end of the road where it turned back into town, there sat an old house. When my brother Jim and I stepped through the front door, I saw something jump at me, so I was headed out the door! The lady said that she had the monkey on a leash and that it wouldn't hurt me.

"Would you like to see him play in the tree outside?" she asked. "Yes," I said.

We walked over to edge of the road by the tree, where a rope had been tied to the tree. The husband of the woman got hold of the rope, and the monkey jumped to the man's shoulder and started swinging out over the highway, State Road 52. He went back and forth until he was high in the air. Then he let go of the rope and dropped into the tree branches. He jumped down, ran up the hill, and did it again, over and over. It was fun to watch him playing with the rope and the trees. After they left, it was our turn to use the rope, but we didn't drop into the tree like the monkey. We were dumb, but not that dumb to drop into the scratchy branches!

Down on Eighteenth and Monon Streets, there was a building that housed Seyfer's Potato Chip trucks, in the basement. On the weekend, Joe, Jim, Lynn, and I, lowered a rope to let Lynn through a side window that was open to let out the trucks' exhaust fumes. It was big enough to let Lynn down to the floor and go into the parked trucks and get out some bags of old chips that were left overnight. He would bring them to the window and hand them up, and we would haul him up on the rope. Then we'd go home and share them with everyone. But Mom said that we were not to go around the chip building anymore, that what we had done was out-and-out stealing.

My time living on the north end was coming to an end. What I didn't know was that our family was splitting up, and my world would be turning upside down. My father and mother were getting a divorce, and the kids were going in all different directions. My older brother Sonny was killed in a motorcycle accident when I was five years old. I remember going to see him at Soller-Baker Funeral Home, which at the time was located on Fourth Street in Lafayette. They ushered us in the side door, and I saw him lying in the coffin. I didn't understand what was going on; to me he looked like he was just sleeping. Then they ushered us back out the side door. The oldest brother was gone forever. If he had stayed alive, he might have taken care of us kids, and kept us all together. Now there were eight of us left. Time was working on our family. The clock doesn't stop for anyone. When you are born, time starts running for you. You don't know where it will take you.

Some of us were going to the Cary Home for Children. The older boys, Gordon and Dick, were too old to go to the home. They would try to get into military service. It sounded too cold to me. Dad left and we stayed with Mom, until the welfare came to get us. But Jim, Joe, and I ran away to where Dad was staying at Mrs. Nugent's house, north Fifth Street.

When we got there, I thought Dad would be glad to see us, but he called the Welfare people to come and get us! What a blow that was to Jim. He was angry because he had thought he could stay with Dad. But Dad didn't want any of us. We went back to Mom's house until the next day.

My sister Marquita and Jim were headed to the Cary Home. Lynn and Hazel would go and live with different people in different towns where we couldn't find them. Hazel was only two years old. Her first name and last name were to change, to make it harder for us to locate her. Lynn would come to the Cary Home over a year later.

Joe and I, (Bill) were sent to the country. The Welfare thought that would be the best place for us, so we couldn't run away, because we wouldn't know where we were. We would stay there until my sixth birthday. Then we would both go out to the Cary Home.

One of my jobs when I was out in the country was to take care of the chicken coop. The farmer's wife showed me how to get the eggs, first thing in the morning after we got up. She would walk up to the hen that was sitting on the nest, put her hand under the hen, and pull out the eggs. Then on to the next one, then the next one, until she had them all.

The next day it was my turn. As I stepped through the door, all the hens looked at me as if to say, "Who are you?" And they gave me the evil eye. When I started to reach under the first one, she had pecked me before I could get my hand under her. I pulled it back as fast as I could! I looked at them with a hard look, but they were giving me an even harder stare.

I went back up to the porch, picked up one egg that was left over in the basket, and walked back to the coop. I opened up the door and stepped in, and there they were giving me the evil eye again. I showed them the egg, and dropped it on the floor. You would have thought that they were shot out of a cannon; that's how fast they flew to get at the egg. I walked over and picked up the eggs as fast as I could. When they jumped back onto their nests after they had there morning meal, they looked all over for their eggs, but no eggs.

My life on the farm was easy for the rest of my stay, at least when it came to the chickens. The day came for my sixth birthday, August 4, 1947. The next day, we said our good-byes and loaded up into the welfare lady's car and headed to the Cary Home. As we looked back at the farmer and his wife as they stood waving goodbye, I couldn't help but think back to Lynn and Hazel, as we stood next to the hedge when my sister and brother were loaded up in the car. As the welfare lady drove down the road and they were crying as they were looking out the back window at us, just standing there. Mom with tears in her eyes, she couldn't do anything about the break up, but stand there and watch the car drive off, with two little faces looking back at her and crying. And in the end, my father liked all of his habits, more than his kids. Who was the problem? It was the self.

When we looked at the building, it was the first time I noticed that it was large and all brick. The left side looked just like the right side. The entrance was large and had a hanging light from the center ceiling. It had a large door made of glass and wood. The welfare lady opened the door and led us into a place where Marquita, Jim, Joe, and I would be starting a new life. Lynn came to the home about a year and a half later. Hazel was adopted, and later Jim found out where she was living.

Jessie's Kids honors Cary Home's namesake

File photo

Frank and Jessie Levering Cary

Supporters of Cary Home for Children on South 18th Street sang "Happy Birthday" last month to Jessie Levering Cary, on her 145th birthday.

The new idea to form Jessie's Kids Foundation this year was another good way to sing it. Jessie, as her obituary had declared in 1927, had been "prominent in charity work." She had sat at local public school desks, and at Purdue University, then had taken a finishing course in a seminary in Philadelphia.

Her parents had been Abraham and Amelia Levering. Levering & Company sold men's hats, caps and gloves down South Third. Abe also ran a wholesale place on Columbia before he accepted a vice presidency at Lafayette Savings Bank.

In November 1892, when she was 27, Jessie married a 34-year-old lumber buyer for the old Lafayette Railroad Car Works at Second and Alabama. He was Frank Cary.

The Car Works nearly failed in the 1890s. Cary left Car Works to take over, reorganize and run the Barbee Wire and Iron Works at Second and South.

The Barbee people had supplied metal parts for the railroad cars. Under Cary's direction Barbee began turning out fences and other wrought iron doo-dads you still see on top of old barns and homes.

Iron crests in those days stood high on many a rooftop. Frank Cary made a pile of money that way, and retired in 1921.

Frank and Jessie Cary named their only son Franklin Levering Cary in 1893.

But the boy of 19 – promising student, St. John's Episcopal choir boy – died of a ruptured appendix in 1912.

Frank and Jessie gave Purdue University $50,000 for a men's dormitory on West Stadium Avenue, a venue we know today as the Franklin Levering Cary Hall complex or, simply Cary Hall.

After Jessie died in 1927 Frank gave the Boy Scouts a 44-acre farm along the Middle Fork of Wildcat Creek east of Lafayette off Indiana 26. The farm since has been improved and enlarged until today we know it and use it as Franklin Levering Cary Camp.

Jessie's obituary said she had given generously to charities in Lafayette and elsewhere, particu-larly educational philanthropies.

Jessie had been a member of St. John's Church and the Marquis de Lafayette Chapter of the Daughters of the American Revolution.

West Lafayette writer Joan Marshall has documented Tippecanoe County's swelling needs for better places for orphaned or otherwise troubled children.

The first shelter had been the County Poor Farm, north of West Lafayette, opened in 1837.

The Poor Farm preceded a Lafayette Industrial School, a Children's Home, the St. Joseph Orphanage and Manual Training Center, a Home for the Friendless, a Rescue Mission and a Women's Christian Home.

In 1929, told about the county's rising needs, Frank Cary, with Jessie's good works in mind, put up $45,000 in her memory.

So Jessie Levering Cary Home for Children opened at 2130 S. 18th St. on Nov. 30, 1930.

With Jessie's good works still in mind, Cary Home's main support group has reinvented and renamed itself after 80 years.

Think of it now as "Jessie's Kids." Help it, and you can sing "Happy Birthday," too.

My older sister
Marquita Holsclaw

Mark ↓ and her friends

Cary Home Children

Front of Cary Home for Children

Back of cary Home

Boys working on side of hill

Cary Home for Children

18th Street South

25

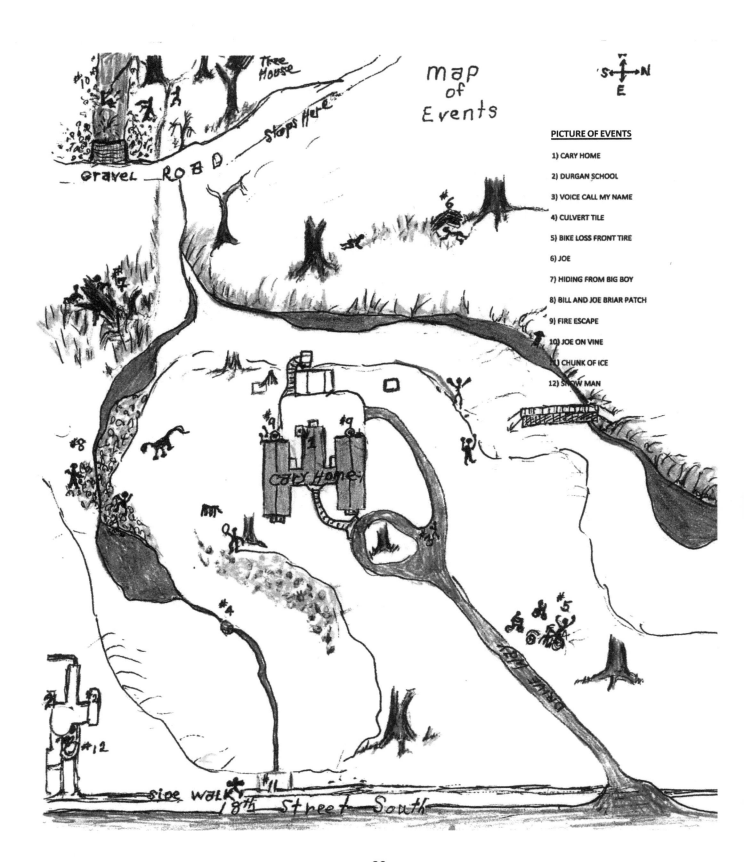

Map of Events

PICTURE OF EVENTS

1) CARY HOME
2) DURGAN SCHOOL
3) VOICE CALL MY NAME
4) CULVERT TILE
5) BIKE LOSS FRONT TIRE
6) JOE
7) HIDING FROM BIG BOY
8) BILL AND JOE BRIAR PATCH
9) FIRE ESCAPE
10) JOE ON VINE
11) CHUNK OF ICE
12) SNOW MAN

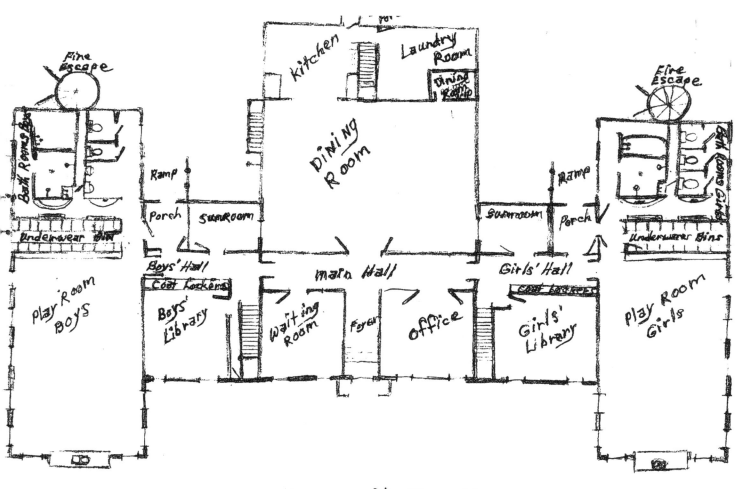

Cary Home 1st Floor Plan

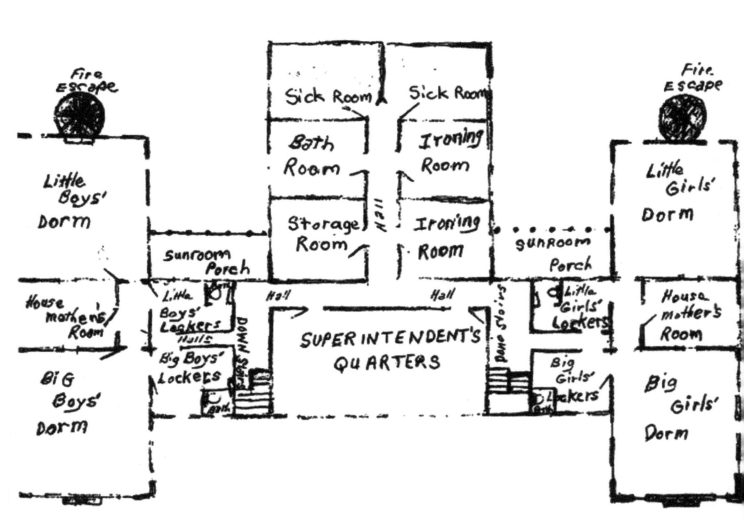

Cary Home 2nd Floor Plan

Life in the Cary Home

When we stopped in front of the Cary Home for Children, I stepped out of the car and picked up our sack of clothes from the trunk of the car. When we had left our home in the north end of town, all of our clothes were put into a grocery bag. All the time we spent on the farm, we never received any new items, and birthdays were just another day.

With the grocery sack in my arms and standing there waiting for the others, the first thing I noticed was that the building was made of bricks and had lots of windows. The left side looked just like the right side, and the door was the central structure and the only way into the front of the building. The front entrance had a large door. It looked like a cathedral arch in the center, with a light hanging on a chain from above. The door had a heavy, oak, wooden frame with panes of glass in rows from the top to the bottom.

The welfare lady, Ms. Stump, held the door open so we could walk into the building. As Joe and I walked through the door and stepped into the foyer, we were now starting a new life; this would be my home for the next twelve years.

Ms. Stump took Joe and me into a room that was a waiting room for guests. It was part of the lobby. She told us to have a seat and wait for her to come back. She was going to see Mr. Sparker, the superintendent, who was in charge of the Home.

While she was gone, Joe and I had a chance to look around. After five minutes, she came back and said to follow her over to the office, where we were introduced to Mr. Sparker. Then she said, "Well, it's all taken care of." She said her goodbye, turned, and left us standing in the office.

Then an older lady came in, and took us out into the hall. She told us to stand close to floor lamp, as she looked into our hair for lice.

We were poor, but our Mother took good care of us, and gave us a bath every night.

Suddenly Marquita and Jim were standing in front of us. It felt good to see family members there! It didn't take long for the news to travel, that there were new kids standing by the office. The housemother, Mrs. Moore, told Jim to take us around, show us the other rooms, and where we would be staying in the dorms at night.

We still had our sack of clothes in our arms. My sister could only go as far as the boys' side sunroom. That was the first room on the right. The boys could only come to the girls' side sunroom. It was on the left side. Whatever you could see from the boys' side, the girls' side was the same, downstairs and upstairs.

We turned, left the sunroom, and walked back out into the boys' hall. There was a long stairway that went up to the second floor, and to the right of the stairs was a small hall that lead to a door, that went to the basement.

The next room that was off the basement hall was a library. Books were lined up on the shelves like *The Hardy Boys*, *Tom Swift*, and many more books. The girls' side had a library with girls' books in it. There were rows of shelves full of hard cover books like *Nancy Drew* and *Little Women*.

Then we moved back into the boys' hall, and as we were walking toward the playroom, on our left, were rows of wooden bifold doors, where you would hang up your winter coats on hooks.

As we walked through double doors, into the playroom, I looked around; this room was long and wide. At the front of the room were two picnic tables, and a pool table. Around the outer walls were chairs that were made of wicker. At the far end of the room was a fireplace, and at the opposite end were long benches. The tops opened up, and they became a storage bin for toys, baseballs, basketballs, footballs, bats, etc. Jim said that you didn't want to do something that would get you into trouble, because that would land you on the bench. The longer you sat there, the harder the seat would get! He said that some kids would sit there for two or three days, not much fun.

Then we turned and walked into a small hall. To our left was a door that was open. When we stepped into the room, there were rows of cubbyholes with names on the front. Here is where you would put your white shirts, underwear, and socks. We still were carrying our sacks. We put our white items in the cubbyholes, and put our names on a piece of tape, so that we'd know which cubbyhole was ours.

Out of the underwear room and into the bathroom, straight ahead and through the door and to your left, were urinals and toilets. Back into the main room, there were two washbasins for your hands and face. One of the washbasins had a step up for smaller kids to reach the water. Behind us were two mirrors on the walls to comb your hair. Around the corner and down a small hall and on the right were two showers. Out of the showers, and at the end of the hall, on the right was a bathtub. We left the bathroom and headed to the upstairs. When we reached the top of the landing and turned to our left, we walked down a hall. There were three doors, but two of the doors were set back out of sight. They led into each dorm. There was a center door, which led to the housemother's room and where she would sleep.

We entered the door on the right. It was the little boys' locker room and dorm. There were a lot of lockers, and a bench in the middle, where we could sit down and put our shoes on.

Jim started opening up locker doors, looking for empty ones. When he found one, he said to me, "This is yours. Put all of your clothes in it." Then he found one for Joe.

Joe said, "How many lockers can we have?"

Jim replied, "You can only have one. In the summer we don't have as many kids, and if you can find one that is empty, you can take it."

Then we stepped from the locker room into the dorm. On each side of the dorm were only beds. At the far end was a fire escape. Jim showed us how it worked: it had two handles at the top, and you had to put your hands on them and push hard, and the doors would pop open. You had to sit and slide down. At the bottom were two more doors, which you had to kick open with your feet. Then you'd be outside, and you would land on the ground.

Some of the beds were not made up. We picked two from the ones that were not made, and Jim showed us how to make our beds.

Then he said, "Every morning, when the bells ring, it's time to get up! The first thing you will do is turn around and make your beds. Then go to your locker and get dressed, and go downstairs to the bathroom and wash up. Then go sit down somewhere, and wait for two bells to ring."

Jim said that he would be on K.P. (Kitchen Police) duties, and he would be in the kitchen helping with the breakfast. He added, "If you don't know what is going on, just ask one of the other boys." As we were leaving the dorm, I noticed a small window in the wall.

Jim walked us over to the dorm that he was in. The dorm was the same as ours, but had no fire escape. Again I noticed that there was a small window in the wall. "What is the purpose of a small window in the wall?" I asked.

"The housemother's sleeping quarters are between the two dorms, and if you make too much noise, she will open the window and tell you to be quiet and go to sleep," Jim replied.

Then he said that we were going to go downstairs, and go outside, and look at the playgrounds! We walked down the stairs to the main hall. On the boys' side, he opened the door, and we stepped out to a porch and a ramp that took us to the backyard. There were a lot of old bikes parked to one side.

The backyard was really big and there were large swing sets. To the left there was a softball field. In the middle of the grounds, and to the right, were a merry-go-round, and monkey bars. By the garage, on each side, was a large sand box.

At the back of the building, by the kitchen, there was a lot made of cement, and a basketball court on one side. There was a backdoor that that you could use, if you had KP duty, to go into the kitchen. Jim said that was where they would ring the three bells. If you were playing outside, it was to let you know when it was time to come in, wash your hands, and get ready to eat.

On the far backside of the ball field and over the hill, and across an open field, was a wood that you could go into and play. There was a creek that ran through it.

This was the type of life that I would be living for the next twelve years. This was my home; I could stay here until I turned sixteen years old, and move out, or stay until I graduated from high school. I made up my mind to get my high school diploma, and then see how the chips fell.

Many years later, they widened the highway and made it larger. Now it was a two-lane highway. I took my car to see how the old neighborhood looked to see if there was any improvement in our old house, and maybe to see the new owner. I asked myself, "What house?" They were all gone: jack the bootlegger, his house, our house, and the other two, all disappeared, lost to the past.

Highland School 1950 2nd Grade ↑ P. 36
Durgan School 1951 3rd Grade ↓ P. 37

School Days

When I first went to the Cary Home for Children, in the summer of 1946, I had to be old enough to go to school. I had to be six years old. My birthday-would be on August 4. The school I would be going to was over by Fourth Street. The name of the school was Highland School, in Lafayette, Indiana. To get to the school we had to walk to it. It was eleven blocks one way. Then at lunchtime we walked back home to eat our lunch. Then back to school. When school was out at the end of the day, we would walk back to the home.

The following year they built a new school, just off Eighteenth Street. It was on the south side of the Cary Home, across the ravine, up the hill. They named it Durgan School. One winter, when I was a sixth grader, it had snowed. I thought that I would build a snowman, between the front two doors, where the kindergarten kids would see it on their way into the school, so I went to school early. I needed to be there early, I was the captain of the patrol. That let me start working on the snowman, and I finished, just as the kids showed up for school. I made my rounds to see if all the other patrol boys showed up, and they were standing by their doors. At noon we went home to eat our afternoon meal, and when I came back after eating lunch, someone had kicked my snowman all down to a pile of snow. I wasn't very happy with what I saw! The next afternoon, we went home to eat lunch, I moved as fast as I could, after being dismissed from the table. I made a beeline to Eighteenth Street, to get a piece of ice from under Eighteenth Street. It was a chunk of ice, hanging down from the drain from above the road. I broke it off from where it was hanging, and carried it on my shoulder, back to the school. I stood it up, and built a snowman around it. It looked as good as new, just like when I had first constructed it. I stepped back to admire it. This time I'd watch for the culprit who had done the dirty deed!

I stood inside of the school, well out of sight, and watched the kids come in the front doors. It didn't take long before a little boy stopped in front of the snowman, made a face of displeasure, and looked around to see if anyone was watching him. He took his foot back and kicked it as hard as he could, then he jumped up and down, holding his foot! He came hopping into school, and he saw me, and knew that I knew he was the one who had kicked it down.

I said to him, "Did you hurt your little footie?" He just gave me a dirty look, and hopped on by me. The moral of this story is, some lessons can hurt in life.

Joe Over the Hill

One of the things my bother Joe liked to do, as well as some of the other boys, was to go over the hill and down into the ravine, where they could hide in a cement culvert and smoke cigarettes.

These normally would be used under the road, to let the water pass, after a rain. This culvert was used to widen the road, but now it was an extra one and was never used. Now it was being used by my brother Joe.

One day I made a slingshot. I needed a small piece of leather, but there wasn't any to be found. Then it hit me: I could use a tongue out of an old shoe, and put two holes in the sides of the tongue. Then I used the shoestrings and tied the string from the shoe in the two holes in the tongue.

I found a rock and put it in the tongue. It couldn't be too big or too small. Then I started swinging it in a circle over my head, and let go of it. The rock hit an old oak tree, twenty yards out in front of me. Whack! What a good shot!

The idea came from the Bible, when David was a boy and he was facing Goliath the giant with only a slingshot. He killed the giant with a rock.

My plan was not to hurt the smokers, but to let them know that I saw them go down the hill, into the cement culvert, to have a smoke.

I picked up a rock, swung it around and around, and let go of one of the strings. It flew high up in the sky, and came down through the trees, crashing and hitting leaves as it came down. You could hear it hitting the rocks in the dried up creek bed, as it ricocheted off the rocks.

I reached down, picked up another rock, and let it fly. It didn't take them long to see me standing up on the hill! With a few choice words, they told me what they were going to do to me. Then I let another rock fly, and down it came through the sycamore trees, hitting right on top of the culvert. The very one they were hiding in.

They came out of their hiding place, running to get me, up the ravine, across the open field. They came to the hill I was standing on, running as fast as their legs could carry them. They were breathless. I said to them, "Too many cigarettes, has shortened your wind, and you're only half way up the hill!"

I turned and headed for the boys' ramp. There were two sets of doors. I went into the one that led to the boy's hall, turned and watched to make sure they were coming.

They saw me, but now there were only three of them. One of them had gone to the back kitchen door, thinking I would be coming out of it.

I was heading for the dining room. I ran to the Main Hall and stopped just short of the doors, watching to make sure they were on their way. They sure were in a hurry to get hold of me! I passed into the dining room, and sat down on the side of the table where Larry Knox sat. Here I could see Joe and his cronies coming in.

Larry was at the head of the table, with a cup of coffee. The housekeeper, with the cook, Mrs. Black, Mrs. Wilson, the girls' housemother, and the janitor, Paris, were all on a coffee break, and smoking cigarettes.

There was no way I could out run all of them! What saved me from Joe and the other boys was, they couldn't see I was baiting them. They were running right behind Joe, too closely, coming down the hall, through the dining room doors. Do you think I was going to let them catch me, and let them work me over? I don't think so!

I knew Larry would be having his afternoon cup of coffee. I heard a commotion out in the front hall, and everyone at the dining room table stopped talking. They turned their attention to see what the commotion was: it was Joe and his cronies! They came running around the corner, coming into the dining room, bumping and shoving into each other. It was too late, because by the time Joe put the brakes on, and saw that Larry was looking at him, the other two boys were running into Joe's back, knocking him down on the floor.

Running in the dining room was a big "no, no." Larry got up and told them to go and sit on the bench. "I'll come over and take care of you later."

What could they say? "We were chasing Bill. Because we were over the hill, down in the ravine smoking cigarettes in the cement culvert." That I was throwing rocks at them, from high up in the air, and I was doing it from a block away from them? I don't think so! All in all, it was mean of me, but I was young, twelve or less, and who would have thought I could use the slingshot that well?

Big Boys in Charge

When I was ten years old, one of the things that the superintendent would do every Friday on the day they would give the housemothers off was that they would put the older boys in charge of the smaller boys. They'd do the same for the girls' side. These were known as the big boys, and they would watch us like a hawk and force their will on us.

After we were done eating our supper meal, around eight o'clock, they would round us up. They wanted us to take showers and get us ready for bed, even though in the summer it was still day light outside. There were sixteen kids and they marched us all into the playroom to get us ready for our showers.

They made us line up, and as we were lining up, it was like a bell went off in our heads. At the same time, we all broke away! I don't know how it worked so well, but we didn't plan it that way. All of us just knew that we were not going to bed that early.

Bob and I made a dash for the stairs. That took us to the little boys' dorm, and some others followed us. We hid in different places; some would hide inside of their lockers, some in the bathroom, and some were under the beds.

Bob and I went to the far end, the last beds against the back wall. He went under the bed on the left, and I went under the bed on my right. These beds were by the fire escape that had doors on it that would open when pushed, if there was a fire. You would sit and slide down, and at the end were two more doors, with a spring bar. When your feet would hit it, it would pop open and let you out, onto the ground outside.

Earlier I would play hide and seek, in the wintertime. I would hide under the beds, and I would hold onto the frame of the bed. When they came into the dorm to find me, I could see their feet as they moved toward me. I would pull myself up and press my whole body against the bed springs. Once I discovered the trick of the beds, I never told anyone about it. They could never find me. The only person I told what to do was Bob.

When the big boys left, we snuck out from under the beds, and opened the fire escape door, very slowly, not to make any noise.

Then we took off our shoes and socks and closed the fire escape doors behind us very softly and slid down to the doors at the bottom.

We could hear two of the boys talking about us, as they stood outside the doors. As we got closer to the doors at the bottom, they were saying, "No one knows where they are!" One of the boys came by, to say that they were in front of the building. Then they all took off to get us.

Then it grew very quiet. We opened the doors very slowly, but the big springs made a squeaking noise. When the doors were open, Bob and I stepped out into the sunset. We put on our socks and shoes. We turned and shut the doors behind us.

To celebrate our freedom, we ran across the playground, over the baseball field, and jumped on home plate! We ran all the way to the hill that went down to the creek, at the bottom of the ravine. Just as we were getting ready to go down the hill, we heard the big boys yell, "They're going over the hill!"

We leaped faster and headed down the hill. With adrenaline pumping we jumped the creek, ran into the tall weeds, and through the weeds to an old tree that a storm had blown over. That was our hiding place; the main trunk was all gone, just the base was left.

We were hiding where we could get a good view of them, as they were coming over the hill. They came running by like rabbits being chased by a fox right past us. They didn't even see us. Six big boys ran down the path in a nice straight line, and into the woods. Then they disappeared out of sight.

Bob and I stepped out from the hiding place, into the open, and crept below the hilltop, so they wouldn't notice us, and we came up behind the garage.

Finally we climbed up the hill and walked up the side walk to the ramp. This happened just in time for the housemother to come out. She wanted to know where we had been.

I said, "We were hiding from the Big Boys." *Slap!* I got slapped across the face. *Slap!* Bob got the same treatment. We didn't care; it was worth it!

"Get in there and get your bath now!" In the end, it was fun, and we pulled one over on the big boys!

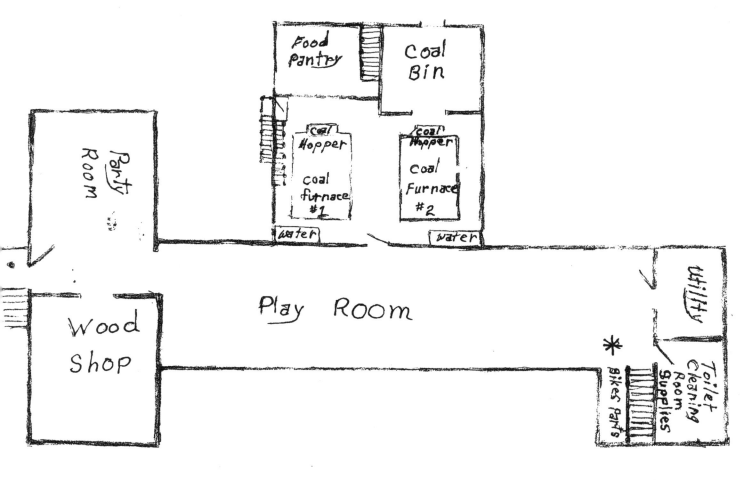

Party
Room

Food
Pantry

Coal
Bin

Coal
Hopper

coal
furnace
#1

Coal
Hopper

coal
Furnace
#2

water

water

Utility

Wood
Shop

Play Room

Toilet
Cleaning
Room
Supplies

Bikes Parts

Basement
Floor Plans

39

Making an Old Bike

When I was thirteen years old, I worked all summer and into winter, mowing lawns, raking leaves in the fall, and shoveling snow. I was trying to save up enough money to buy a new bike. There would be no more old bikes for me!

It was difficult trying to find old, used parts for my old bike. Then I'd see if they would fit on the bike. Often the links that lock the ends of the chain together were missing on the bike chain. To make it work, you would use piece of wire, trying to bring the two links together. This would hold the chain and lock it, so you could pedal the bike. What I had been doing was making a bike out of spare parts.

When I finished the frame, I would go to the basement to find more parts. I needed tires, and tubes for the insides of the tires, preferably the ones that would hold air! However, they all had their problems that I couldn't overcome.

I didn't have money for tubes or tires, because my allowance was only twenty-five cents per week. To solve the problem, I would take two old tires that were worn out, put the worst one on the inside of the rim, and the next one on top of the first one. I had two tires on front and two on the back wheels.

I stepped back and took inventory of my bike. When you looked at the bike, you would see a frame with old tires on it, no fenders on the front or back. It had a seat that was metal only, and most of it was rusted. There was no chain guard over the chain.

If your blue jeans would get caught in the chain, you would have a hard time trying to stop the bike with your good leg. You would need to hold the bike up, so you could move the pedal around until the chain released your pants. The best thing to do was to roll up your pants leg before you got on, to keep it out of the chain and oil.

The brakes were held in place by wire so you could stop the bike. Sometimes the wire would break, and the brakes would lock up. Then you would need to unwind the wheel to release the brake gears, and put new wire on again.

The old bikes would sit out in all kinds of weather, even in the winter. The handlebars had rust all over them, the chrome was just rust. Even if you had a new bike there was nowhere to store it out of the weather.

Well, that was my bike. No one would use my bike. The bottom line was, it was just a heap of rusted junk. The other kids would get new bikes from their divorced parents. This was the way they had to show they still loved them. I had to make do with what I could get my hands on.

The only time my mother came to see me, was to introduce her new husband to me. He was now my stepfather. After ten minutes, they said good-bye, and left. She did say I could come down and see her and Jim, down on the avenue, where they now lived. I put my leg over my old rusted seat, and rode away on my old "new" bike. It worked pretty well for not having any tubes in its tires! It ran on four outer tires. There was no master link to lock and hold the chain together, and no padding on the seat. There was no chrome on the bike. It had all turned to hurtful rust.

Making Fun of My Old Bike

Some of the bigger boys were making fun of my old bike. I had to make it out of used parts. It was the best I could do, with what I had to work with! I told them that this old bike could do things that their bikes couldn't do. They said, "Show us when we come back from the bathroom."

When they went inside, I reached into my pocket, and took out my wrench, to loosen up the front nuts on each side of the front wheel of one of the boy's bikes. I backed away from their bikes and was sitting on my old bike when they came out. They came down the ramp to get to their bikes, laughing at me. "Let's go!" they said.

We rode out the front driveway, in and out of the white rocks that lined the road on both sides.

"Is this the best you can do?" they teased.

I rode over the big oak trees that were in the yard, and I was jumping the roots that were lying on top of the ground. They were laughing at me.

"Easy-peasy," they said. I said, "Watch this!"

I rode over a deep hole, where there used to be an old oak tree that fell over in a storm. This happened long before I was born; now it was a rounded pothole. I took my bike down into it very fast and out the other side. I did a wheelie, coming out the other side, with my front wheel up high in the air. The front tire was spinning like a top!

One of the older boys said, he would show me how it was done! I was sitting on my bike sideways, then the next one was in line to jump. He went down and up, and did his wheelie.

The other boy said, "Let me show you girls how to do it!"

This was the one that was bad-mouthing my old bike. He pedaled as fast as he could go down into the hole and up the other side. He did a big wheelie, but then, oops! His front wheel came off and kept on going, but the fork of the bike stuck in the ground. Over the handlebars he flew! He was sitting on the ground, saying, "I can't believe this! How could this happen?"

I said to him, "Go get your tire, and I'll help you put it on your bike."

He never did find out that I set him up for a great fall.

I said, "You have a very nice bike, but you need to check the bike, before you ride it every time." Nevertheless, sometimes pride goes before a fall, and he just looked at me. What I said went right over the top of his head.

Thinking back on the event, I might have had a small mean streak in me!

The Night the Electricity Went Out

In the Cary Home everything operated off a bell system: the morning wake-up call was four bells. That meant to get out of bed, turn around, and make your bed. Then you'd get dressed, go downstairs, and wash your face and comb your hair. By that time we would hear three bells go off, which were telling the ones that were on KP to get into the kitchen and help with the meal and to set up the tables. The head cook didn't want boys on KP, only girls. That sounded like music to my ears; I didn't want to be on KP either!

The noon meal would start like the morning meal. If you were outside, you would hear a single bell go off, which signaled you to get to the kitchen to help with the noon meal, if you were on KP. After ten minutes, you would hear three bells ring. This meant it was time for everyone to go inside and get cleaned up. In another ten minutes, a bell would ring two times, which meant to get into line so you could go into dining room to eat.

The evening meal had the same number of bells, and we would line by height from the smallest boys first, back to the tallest boys. The girls did the same, smallest to the tallest, girls walking in first to their tables, led by the housemother. There were not as many girls since most of the girls were on KP. Their line was short. The boys came next, led by their housemother. We would stand until we would say grace, then sit down to eat. When we were all done, the first table would carry their plates into the kitchen. If you were on kitchen duty, you would stay and clean up, and then you would have the rest of the time off.

One morning, the housemothers, whose job was to be in charge of the boys and the girls, had to get us out of bed in the middle of the night! We had a storm during the night, and had lost power. There were no lights nor bells to tell us to get up for breakfast. We made our beds, and put our clothes on in the dark. We went downstairs and tried to clean up the best we could in the dark.

After we cleaned ourselves up, and got in line for our breakfast, we marched into the dining room. On each table there were two candles that lit the eating area. When we were finished eating, each table of boys and girls would take their dishes out to the kitchen.

As our table dropped off our dishes, we went out the dining room double doors. Instead of going to the boys' side like we normally would do, we turned to the left. We passed Larry Knox's office, turning our heads to make sure he wasn't in his office. What luck! He was not in there, so we headed to the girls' coat lockers. In the hall, there were four sets of bifold doors. If all the doors were closed, you could see and walk from one end to the other. This is where we'd keep all the coats; you would hang your winter coats up on the coat hooks.

We all stood in our section, waiting for the unsuspecting girls to come by in the dark hallway. I told them not to jump out at the girls until they were about half way down the hall. I looked out through the crack in the door, and two girls were coming our way. When they were mid-way, we popped the doors open on them. They jumped and screamed, and ran into the bathroom to hide!

Then we would wait until another set of girls would come by, and we would pop open the doors and scare them, also! Then we'd close the doors, and it would start over. This was fun for us, but not so much for them! I opened the doors a little way so I could see if any girls were coming out of the main dining room hall, and would let the others know when to get ready to jump out. Sometimes the girls would turn and go up the stairs to the girls' dorm.

It was getting daylight outside; there was enough light that you could see over to the boys' side, and as I stood there with my door cracked, so I could signal our next surprise attack, what I saw was not a very pretty sight. It was the superintendent, Larry Knox! He had been the janitor when I first came to the Cary Home, but now he was the main man! He was a little overweight, short, with bulgy eyes. He kind of looked like a bulldog on a mission, swinging his arms like King Kong!

Coming from the boys' side, his eyes were set on a target. It was too late to warn the others, because by that time, he was in the main hall. All I could do was watch as the doom came down on us. Now he was in the girls' hall, and standing in front of the first set of the bifold doors. He popped open the first bifold doors and pulled out Jerry and Dan. If you could have seen their faces! We thought we knew how to scare the girls, but they discovered what scaring was now! He grabbed the two brothers by the neck, turned them toward the boys' side, kicking them in the rear, and told them to go over to their side of the building where they belonged. They were to sit on the dreaded oak bench; they were crying as they were running to the bench! Larry shut those doors and moved to the next set of doors. He popped them open and grabbed Jim and JC out the same way, with a foot sending them on their way. He closed the locker that they were in, and stepped over to the one that was next to me. Bob was in it; he knew something wasn't right, but what could he do? The impending doom was about to get him! The doors opened. And a hand and arm reached in and pulled him out. The big foot found his rear, and off to the other side he went.

Now it was my turn! I heard the bifold doors shut where Bob had been, and moved over into his place. So when Larry opened my doors, I wasn't there! He looked hard to make sure no one was hiding behind the coats in there, and slammed the doors shut. Then I moved back over where I had been before, and Larry opened the side I had just left. He found no one—nothing there! He closed the doors hard, turned and went to the boys' side to talk to the boys that got caught.

I cracked my door to make sure he didn't turn and look back. Then I slipped out the girls' side, down the ramp, and around to the boys' side. I sneaked up the ramp, came through the door on the right, and into the bathroom. I could hear him yelling at them, telling them that they were going to sit on the bench for the rest of the day, with no talking, and they could only get up to go to the bathroom. To make matters worse, for the next two weekends they were going to cut weeds in the ravines.

My friends never informed on me. When I could talk to them, they wanted to know how I got away with it! I told them that I would step across to the locker that was next to me after Larry closed it, and then back to the one I had been in. Of course they said it wasn't fair!

I told them, "In time of need when fear and doom is looking for you, you need a plan that works!"

Cary Home Highlights

Over a period of time, I grew older, but still was sleeping in the little boys' dorm. When you turned thirteen years old, you moved over to the big boys' dorm. One of my best friends was Bob Gordon; we both were waiting to get old enough to move to the big boys' dorm. Then we could stay up for one more hour longer!

To have something to do, we would go down into the woods, and work on the tree house: Bob and the England brothers, JC and Bill. By this time, my youngest brother Lynn was living at the Cary Home and old enough to go to school. Like me, when our family broke up, he was too young to go to the Cary Home. He also needed to be six years old. He was about two years younger than me. Now he could come with us to the tree house.

The only way to get to the woods was across the back yard, then to follow a path through the weeds over by the road. This road went down a small hill to where the water came out of a sewer. It must have rained during the night, because the opening from the sewer had a lot of water and waste coming from the overflow.

There was a lot of water going down the creek. One of the boys yelled, "There's a floater!" We all picked up rocks, trying to sink it, but it was moving along very fast. Someone hit it square on, and it smashed up into a brown mess. The turd was gone!

We were looking for a vine that would be heavy enough to hold our weight, close to the creek, where we could swing out over the water, just to have fun swinging on a vine. The vine was also needed to have a place to cross the creek when we needed to get to the other side and the water was too high to cross on foot.

We found a vine that was growing up a tree to the top. The root of the vine was alive and growing in the ground. We had a pocketnife that was used to cut it, so it would move and let us swing out over the water.

Carefully checking to make sure it would hold our weights, we would put all the weight of four bodies on the vine. Then we moved higher up the hill to see if we could swing out over the water and back to the bank. We ran faster and faster, until we were at our limits. Over time the vine got weaker, because we had cut the main root that nourished it. We did not realize that someone could get hurt.

All of us took turns swinging out over the water; we were having lots of fun with the vine! Then my older brother Joe showed up and wanted to swing on the vine too.

He was going to show us how to make it—in other words, how to conquer the vine. He was going to show off.

He went up the hill, much farther than we would, to the point of no return. Down the hill he came, and right at the bottom, where your body leaves the ground, the vine would take on the weight of his body. At that time, the vine would normally take you out across the creek. The creek was mostly sewer waste from the hard rain runoff.

Right at the lifting point, the vine broke! Joe, still holding the vine, went into the wastewater facefirst. When he stood up, we were all having a hearty laugh at him. He was dripping wet with water, and when he stood up, holding his arm, he said, "Something is wrong with my arm; I think I broke it!"

He did break his arm and had to go to the hospital. He had to have it set in a cast. To this day, he carries a scar about six inches long, after he got the cast off. It is a reminder of how he got it.

While Joe was getting his arm set, Lynn was tying the vine to the tree at the top. After tying knots in the vine, we were back in business and having fun again!

Jerry and the Sled

It was Saturday, and to my thirteen-year-old mind, the best day ever, because there was no school. I looked out the window and saw that it had snowed during the night. There was new snow on the ground and the sun was shining and the sky was bright blue.

After we had our breakfast, we had to strip the floors on the girls' side, the main entrance, and the boys' side. The floors in these rooms were made from polished rock. We had to strip the floor down with a buffer pad, apply new wax, and after that, we used fans so the floor would dry faster. We polished the dried wax with the buffer so the floor would have a high shine. After we were done, we would have the rest of the day free. Then Larry would give us our allowance for the week; mine was thirty cents.

I am now a big boy, I have moved across the hall into the big boys' dorm. I can do more than just dusting, and picking up items off the floor, like running the buffer and doing heavier work. Sometimes I would go down to the lowest level and put coal in the hopper to keep the coal burning for the furnace, heating the building in the wintertime. I would also carry out the ashes to the back of the garage, and dump them over the hill.

With new snow on the ground, it was time to find the snow sled. I searched all over for it, and found it in the garage hiding in a corner of the building. When I got it out into the light, I could see the runners were all rusted. I needed to clean them up before it would slide down the hill smoothly.

I found an old rag and some oil with which I could clean up the runners, after I polished the sled. I put the sled on the snow to see how it would slide along; it didn't take me long to get it ready for the hills!

The hill the boys would go down was on the girls' side. The hill we used went straight down, over two bumps, and jumped the creek. We would fly through the air and into the hillside that would stop the sled in its tracks!

I tried it out first, but it didn't go as fast as I would have liked it to. It just made it across the creek, but after going down the hill six or more times, it was going faster and faster.

Jerry asked, "Can I take a turn?"

"Sure," I said, "but you need to bring the sled back to me at the top of the hill." I handed it to him. Jerry would do things to aggravate me; he had lots of fun trying to rub you the wrong way.

He was going fast, up and over the two bumps, jumped the creek and hit the hill like a rock. On the other side, he rolled off the sled, and I could tell he was hurting a little. He was coming back without the sled; he left it on hill!

I yelled at him to bring the sled back to me. By now, he was about sixty feet away from me, laughing at me.

He said, "Get it yourself, if you want it!"

I reached down, picked up some snow, made a snowball, and threw it at him. He just stepped out of the way and I missed him. I reached down and made another one, and I packed it very hard.

I told him, "Get the sled now!"

Jerry put his arms in the air and waved them back and forth. "Fine," he said.

"Think you can hit me?" as he was laughing.

I looked at him and let the snowball fly. Again he just stepped out of the way, and he was singing a little song, "Nah, nah, ne, nah, nah, you can't hit me!" It was accompanied by a little dance, his hands up to his face, with his tongue sticking out, moving his body back and forth.

He was right. No matter how hard I threw the snowball, he was far enough away to move out of the way, all he had to do was to just step to one side. However, I had a plan in my mind.

I said to him, "Are you going to go and get the sled?" His answer was in a song, "Oh, no, oh, no, noooooo!"

This time when I went down to make a snowball, I made two! I stood up with one in my hand, and let it fly. Just as before, he just stepped to one side. Then I went down and made another one and stood up with one in each hand, but I cupped one so he couldn't see it.

I stood up, looked at him standing with his arms up in the air and moving around, like a mad man. I threw the snowball in my right hand, high into the air, and as he was watching it come down, he said, "Oh, no It's going to hit me in the head. I'm so scared," as he was doing his little dance. Then I put the other snowball in my right hand. Let go of the other one straight at him, as hard as I could, and it was on target! It hit him on the side of the head, and then the one coming down from the air hit him on top of the head!

He was having a hard time believing that he was hit. Now it was my turn to sing, "Nah, nah, ne, nah, nah! I hit you!" I turned around and walked back to the home, singing a little song. "This is the best day ever, ever, Ever!" By the next day, we were friends again, talking and laughing, just like nothing happened, everything was in the past.

Dinosaur in the Woods

One of the things I would do in the winter, when we had our first big snow, was to get a bunch of kids to help make a snowman. This time I had no helpers, so I thought I would try to make something by myself.

"What could I build? Think, I know! I'll make a large, large dinosaur!" How was I going to make a huge dinosaur with no helpers, and give it a long neck, and a tail as long as the neck? Luckily, the snow was right: nice and wet and heavy. It was just right for creating a large snowball.

I started rolling a snowball from the top of the playground, and down a small incline, towards the woods. The construction of the body was first; it would require at least six large snowballs. I put the first one in place; it was almost as tall as me, five feet tall. Now there was one in place and five to go!

As I went back to the top of the playground, I turned and looked at my snowball sitting by itself. I reached down and picked up some more snow, to make the second snowball, then put it on the ground and started rolling it into a bigger snowball.

I had to make it as big as the one down in the woods. Starting at the top, making sure I was going down the hill to the woods, I was putting my last large snowball place, when I stopped to look up at the playground. The snow was about gone! It had taken a massive amount of snow to build the body of the dinosaur.

I stopped and looked around for more snow. I saw it way over by the baseball diamond. I would start working on the tail next. I rolled one large snowball, and when I stopped at the dinosaur, I chopped the snow up into small pieces, for the neck and the head.

I used old sticks that fell off the trees, to help hold the pieces together. I put the sticks into the body, shoved the snowball onto the stick, and then another one. I used one final snowball for the oversized face and added a smile on it.

I needed the sticks to help hold up the neck. The work with the snow was done, and when I looked around I saw that there wasn't a lot of snow left on the ground in the baseball diamond area.

My next job was to find a bucket, and to fill it up with water. I also needed a cup to throw water on the dinosaur, so it would turn to rock-hard ice. This was necessary because with the large number of kids who lived at the Home, one or two would get in their mind to kick it in, and destroy all my work. Sometimes you need to think outside of the box, to solve a problem before it happens!

Before the bells went off, telling us to make our beds, and then to get dressed and go downstairs, I looked out the window. There was my white dinosaur down in the woods! To make the effect even better, there was a fog rolling across and through the woods. I woke up some of the other kids to look at it; they thought it was amazing.

It was a lot of work; it took half a day with no help. It has become a long-lasting memory that will be with me forever.

Under Attack at My Fort

School was out; it was summertime. Cary Home had a lot of land, about thirty acres of land, and most of it was covered in weeds. I was busy behind the ravines, where there had been a garden in the late thirties.

This was when they learned to work for their food, and then take care of the land. If you did something wrong or broke a rule, one of the punishments was to have you cut weeds. The front of the Cary Home sat on a little island, surrounded on three sides by weed-covered ravines.

There was a 60 foot bridge that went across the north ravine. One day I was out in the weeds working on my fort. I was digging a hole in the ground, large enough for two or three people to sit in it or hide. To the right of the fort was a large oak tree.

As I was minding my own business, digging the hole, I noticed out of the corner of my eye my brother Joe crawling on his hands and knees, trying to sneak up on me. I acted like I didn't see him, as he got closer to me. He was trying to stay low to the ground, like a lion sneaking in for the kill.

I stopped working. Then I stood up like I needed to stretch. He would put his head down on the ground to hide his face, as if that would keep me from seeing him! I would stand up and stretch, and then I would go back to work. Joe would crawl closer to me, until he was just the right distance from me. Just the right distance for what I had in mind to take care of him. It was time for me to go into action. When I stood up, he had put his face down into the ground..I stepped over and got hold of a hand full of weeds, which when I pulled them out of the ground, all of the dirt stayed on their roots. I turned around and let it fly through the air, not thinking it would hit him, but it landed right on top of his head!

Up and out of his hiding place he came running after me. *Mad* is not the word I would use, shoving dirt off his face, using many of his choice words! Off I went with my legs headed down the ravine and back up the other side, to the Cary Home. No bridge for me to cross over on, Joe was too close to me, right on my tail!

I crossed the playground on the girls' side. Then I headed down across the boys' side, and into the ravine, jumping high into the air. As I arrived, there was a nest of bramble bushes in front of me. I was stepping on the thistles and thorns so they wouldn't grab me and stick me, so they wouldn't slow me down and bring me to a full stop. Next, I crossed to the other side, thirty feet in all, where this patch of thistle ran from the culvert to where the boys liked to smoke, to the bottom, and on around to the next ravine.

I turned around to see what Joe was going to do. I was standing on one side of the thistles and Joe on the other side, still red in the face and very mad. He jumped right into the thorns! Joe thought he was going to run through the thorns, but after about six feet in, he came to a complete stop. Now he was trying to back out, because the thorns had stuck to his blue jeans and some of his skin.

"Ouch! Ouch!" And some more choice words. Finally, Joe got out, not as mad as he was before, and the red face was gone. The only thing left was pain.

Joe said to me, "You will have to come up sometime. I'll be waiting for you on the ramp, with some of my friends!"

It was getting about time to eat: before the words were out of his mouth, we could hear three bells go off. That was a signal to go inside and clean up. Joe turned and started walking up to the Cary Home. He left me standing on the far side of the thistles.

It was a problem for me, but I had a plan. I headed along the ravine, staying low over the hillside. This way they couldn't see me moving closer to the back of the building. I came up behind the garage, and when I peeked out from the side of the garage, I could see the boys' ramp. Sure enough, Joe was sitting on the ramp rail with his friends, true to his word.

I went over the hill again, going on around to the girls' side where the bridge was. They couldn't see me come up as I ran across the road. Staying up against the girls' wall on the outside, I was moving to the front of the building. It was a good thing that there was a lot of greenery, so they couldn't see me moving along the sides of the building.

Even the front had greenery all over it. I stayed next to the building and came out in front of the main entrance, looking in the front door. I opened the door slowly, and walked up the first two steps, staying against the wall, and then through the opening to the front hall. To my relief, no one was there! I was now in the main hall, looking into the dining room, and some of the girls were setting the tables.

If Larry saw me in the front hall, I would be sitting by myself, in the boy's playroom, on a hard bench for a week, cutting weeds for a week.

I moved very slowly against the wall, headed to the boys' side. No one was in the halls. It was clear on the girls' and the boys' side. What luck! I was now standing on the boys' side, and there wasn't anyone who saw me coming into the front entrance hall.

I looked out the window, from the sunroom, where I could see the boys' ramp, and there was Joe, still waiting with his friends, sitting on the rail, guarding the ramp. They also guarded the two doors one which led into the bathroom, and the other which led into the boys' hall, by the coat lockers.

About that time two bells sounded. Before anyone could see me, I was up the stairs standing on the top landing, looking over the railing. This way I could see the last boy go into the main hall. I also saw Joe turning and looking around to see if I was getting in line to eat, with an evil smile on his face.

The house mother was standing next to the first boy in the front row. She started leading the line in, when everyone was quiet. Just as the last boy passed through the double doors, like a flash, I was down the stairs, and got in line just as the last boy passed into the dining room. I walked to my table and seat, and we said our prayer. I looked over at Joe; he couldn't believe his eyes! How could I have made it to my table in time to eat? My plan worked, but Joe's plan didn't.

When we were dismissed from our tables to take out our dishes to the kitchen, I passed Joe on his way out of the kitchen. Joe hit me in the arm, which meant that everything was "even," and I smiled to myself. It was over, and I was free to walk unmolested until the next event. All was good in the Carry Home.

The Wrong Family for Me

When I was ten years old, there was a family that wanted to have me to come out to their family farm for the summer vacation. I was looking forward to going. The day finally came when school was coming to an end.

I could tell there was a problem when the husband was the only one who came to pick me up. When we arrived at the farm, we put my suitcase in the bedroom upstairs for me. I was shown around the farm yard; and there were chickens, pigs, cows, cats, and a horse.

The farm had a barn, garden, and farm equipment to work the fields, but no farmer's wife. The husband said his wife was a little under the weather. "But I do have a job for you. It's not hard. I'll show you how to do the job. We need to get some corn in a bucket, and then go into the barn yard and feed the pigs and the horse."

When the animals saw us with bucket of corn, they came running to get at it. The farmer said, "You need to hold the bucket up high so the animals won't knock it out of your hands!" When we fed the animals, we put the bucket back by the corn, where we could find it the next time.

We moved over to the chicken coop, and on the way we picked up a bucket and put some chicken feed in it. We walked into the chicken yard and coop, where most of the hens were waiting to be fed.

Then the farmer said that it was my job to feed the barnyard animals, get the eggs in the morning, and put them on the back porch.

"Do you think you can do it?"

I said, "Yes, sir!"

The next morning came, and the farmer said to me, "Did you hear my wife crying in the middle of the night?"

I said, "No, I didn't hear a thing, I was sleeping."

"Well, if you hear her tonight, come into our room and crawl into bed with her, and she'll think you're her son. Now go feed the animals. I'll fix our breakfast by the time you are done."

So I went out, picked up the bucket, and put corn in it for the pigs and horse. I came to the gate and climbed over the fence to the yard, and the pigs were all over me, so I held the bucket up high. I got an ear of corn and I threw it as far out in front of them as I could, and they took off after it. I gave some corn to the horse; then I dumped the rest on the ground, and it was a free for all: each pig was living up to its name!

I returned to the back porch and picked up an egg, and headed to the chicken coop. I opened up the door and the hens were sitting on their nests, watching me as if I was chicken hawk and to see what I was going to do. Like on the other farm where I had gathered eggs, I showed them the egg. I held it up for them to see, and then I dropped it to the floor, and the game was on! They flew out of their nests to get the broken egg. I raced to their nests and got every one of their eggs before they could get back to their nests. I won hands down!

I walked back into the kitchen and the farmer wanted to know how things went. "No problems," I said, and sat down to eat my breakfast. "I thought to myself, "Still no wife." When I was done with my meal, I went out and walked around the farm. The farmer came and wanted to know if I would like to go into town with him, and I said, "Sure."

By the time we got back, it was time to eat. We had sandwiches and milk, and I watched some TV. There was not much to watch, so I went to bed early.

The next morning I hopped out of bed, turned around and made my bed, and went downstairs to feed the animals. When I entered the kitchen I saw my suitcase sitting there.

The farmer said to me, "Pack your things." I was going back to the Cary Home. I knew he was mad at me because I didn't hear his wife crying during the night. Even if I had, I wouldn't come in and act like I was her son.

When we arrived at the Cary Home, he let me out and drove off. I turned and walked into the building carrying my suitcase. Larry was in his office, and when he looked up he said, "What did you do now?"

So I told him that the farmer had lost his son in a car accident and his wife cried all the time that I was there. And that at night, when I heard crying he wanted me to come into their room and act like I was their dead son. I couldn't be her dead son! During all the time I was there I never saw his wife.

After talking to Mr. Knox, he understood, that was the real reason I was wanted on the farm. I felt sorry for their loss, but not in that sense. That family was not for me.

New Bike

Working all summer outside of the Cary Home, mowing grass, and in the wintertime, by shoveling snow, I saved up enough money for a new bike.

Larry Knox said he would take me downtown to get my new bike at Montgomery Wards. I was short one dollar twenty-five cents. Back in those times, they didn't charge sale tax on everything that was sold in a store.

Larry said we would wait until I made some more money mowing grass, and we would come back, I looked down at my feet and my heart felt like it was sitting on my feet.

The salesman knew that I lived at the Cary Home for Children. He said, "Wait a minute, I think I have the money in my pocket that you need." Sure enough he had more than I needed! I thanked him like I never thanked a person who was so kind in my hour of need.

It was my first bike, a Schwinn with knee-action springs, and everything on it was new. I got on it and rode it up and the down driveway, the black-top road that led to the Cary Home.

The lunch bell rang just as I pulled up on my new bike to park it, and then I saw how sad my old bike looked. In the end, I would give it to someone else. To them it would look "new."

I was thirteen years old when I first bought my new bike. About a week later, my brother and I went to see the superintendent, who was in charge of the Cary Home. It was Saturday; we got our allowance. We wanted to see if we could go to the movies downtown, at the State Theater on Fifth Street, most of the kids called it The Old Bloody Bucket. The first thing he asked us was, "Do you have the money?"

We showed him our twenty-five cents to get in. "Get out of here but be back by five o'clock sharp." It was one o'clock and the movies stared at one thirty sharp.

We ran out of Cary Home as fast as we could. I let Joe jump on the handlebars of my new bike, out of the driveway and onto Eighteenth Street, headed downtown.

Up to Kossuth Street, turned left and down to Eighth Street and turned right, two blocks and we were at the top of a very steep hill. We were in a hurry to get to the bottom. I was peddling as fast as I could, the tears in my eyes were running on the side of my face, and our hair was flying.

I would say we were going about thirty-five miles an hour, but there was trouble afoot. We were not more than halfway down the hill and then a train came a flying across the tracks. Immediately I put on the brakes, but that wasn't slowing us down very much.

Joe saw that we were in trouble, and to help us to slow down, he jumped off the handlebars and put his hands on bars to hold on, as he put his shoes on the black top to act as breaks to slow us down. When we came to a stop, we were about three feet from the train!

I got off the bike. Joe was already off and I was backing the bike back up the hill away from the train. You could feel the wind from the train blowing on us as it was moving by. That's how close we were to it.

When Joe had jumped off the handlebars, I laid the bike down in the middle of the road, and Joe was jumping up and down, and running around. I thought he was happy that we didn't get hit by the train. That would have been the end of us.

So I said to him, "The way you are running around and jumping up and down, I can tell that you are glad we didn't get run over by the train."

"No, that's not it. My feet are burning up!" Joe sat down on the curb, and pulled his shoes off, and rubbed his feet with his hands to try and cool them off. Then Joe showed me his shoes, the souls and heels of the shoes where almost gone.

Then I said, "We need to move if we are going to get to the movies on time." We jumped on the bike and on down the hill. We went to Main Street, down Main to Fifth Street, half way down the block, there was the Old Bloody Bucket. I locked my bike up.

We went up to the ticket booth, and paid for our tickets, it was very dark inside. We stopped until we could see where we were going, to a seat that wasn't worn out, and we found two. They were showing the news reel, and a cartoon, then Superman Number Seven, then the Main show, King Kong.

We arrived back at the Cary Home at 4:30 p.m. I parked my bike and locked it up. I looked it over to make sure it was ok, and it checked out fine. What a day!

Joe and the Gum

I remember when I was in sixth grade with Joe. Even though he was my older brother, it was a split class. I was in the fifth grade, and Joe was in sixth grade. We were working on our reading workbooks, when Ms. Henderson said to Joe, "What is that you have in your mouth, Joe?"

"Gum," he replied between chews.

She ordered him to throw it into the waste basket, so he got up and threw it into the wastebasket, and went back to his seat at the back of the room.

About ten minutes later, the teacher said to Joe, "Joe, what's that in your mouth?"

He said, "Gum."

This time she took the wastebasket to him and made sure he threw it away! Then she moved him up right next to her desk. That became his permanent spot in the classroom for the rest of the year.

He became a seventh grader at Sunnyside School. Eventually, when he turned sixteen, he could drop out of school. He decided he wasn't going to school anymore. This decision meant that he was out of the Cary Home, and he had to move in with our mom and stepdad, Jim McCord.

Mortuary Business

I was seventeen years old, and I still lived at the Carry Home for Children, and it was Christmastime.

School would be out for about two weeks because of the holiday break. When you lived at the Carry Home, most of the days were like all other days: we would do our chores, and when we had free time, we could go outside, or read a book.

One day, Larry Knox called me into his office. Larry said that there was a man who would like to have some help over the holidays with his work. He needed help with the business that he was in, and that he lived up in Winamac, Indiana.

I asked, "How long would I be up there?"

He said I would be there for two weeks, and if I liked it there, I might stay there, go to school, and have a good job when I graduated from high school.

I asked, "What kind of work is he in?"

Mr. Knox hesitated and then said, "He has a mortuary business."

"I said, I don't think I would like that job."

Mr. Knox said, "Why don't you go up there and try it for two weeks. You may like it more than you think."

This was his way of saying, "You are going to go up there, and try it out. It may be something you might like to be in, and if not, you can come back, and finish going to high school here."

Later that day I was called into the office of the superintendent again. In front of the office desk was a suitcase. It was not a grocery sack, like all the other times, that I used for my clothes.

Mr. Knox said to me, "Here is your suitcase. Go and put your clothes in it, because you will be there for two weeks. He will be here at five this evening to pick you up. Make sure you are ready!"

Then 5:00 p.m. came, and as sure as the nose on your face follows you around, there he was. I picked up my suitcase and said goodbye to Mr. Knox, and out the front door we went. Sitting in the front driveway, was a black hearse. We got into the black hearse and headed out of the driveway. Then we turned right on to Eighteenth Street and down to Teal Road. Finally we went over to State Road 52 south.

I asked, "Where are we going?"

The undertaker said we were going to Indianapolis, to pick up a deceased body that passed away during the night.

When we arrived at the hospital, we went to the back of the hospital, to the loading docks, and went inside to pick up the body. It was naked and had an ID tag on its toes. It was waiting for us in the hallway of the basement. We rolled the body out to the hearse, lifted it up, and put it into the back of the hearse.

One of the first things I learned from this job: what it was like to pick up dead weight.

On the way back to Winamac, we stopped in Lafayette to get a sandwich. He told me to watch the body and wait in the hearse while he went inside to get the food. I can say I didn't look over my shoulder more than I needed to.

When we got to Winamac, it was very late. I was told to go up to my room that was on the third floor. To get there I had to go up the backstairs. When I started up the stairs, the lights did shine on the second floor, but no lights for third floor at all! When I finally got to the top of the third floor stairs, I walked straight ahead and bumped into the door. I reached inside of the room, felt the light switch, and turned the light on. I saw that there was a bed: a single one with a night table. So I put my suitcase on the end of the bed, and put on my pajamas.

Most of the time that I was there we would go around to other mortuaries, to look at some of the bodies. I learned how the undertakers fixed the damage that was caused by gunshots, suicides, and car accidents.

They would talk about how nice a cosmetic job they did on the faces, or how it covered up so well. They were proud when they could have an open casket, and not a closed one.

One night I was climbing up the back stairs. When I came to the top on the third floor stairs, I stepped onto the landing, and I heard some children playing in the empty room. This room was to the right of me.

I thought to myself, "What are the twins doing in that room, laughing and playing? They should be in their beds down on the second floor, but now they were up here! I put my hand inside and flicked on the light switch. As I stepped inside of the room, there were no children. There wasn't anything in that room: No furniture, just an empty room. No one was there!

My stay at that mortuary was for only two more days. For the rest of the time, when I would go up the stairs to sleep at night, I left the lights on in my room all night. Out at the Cary Home I was considered a big boy, but not now. If they only knew!

So when I got dropped back off at the Carry Home, the first thing the superintendent did was to call me into his office.

When I walked in, he said, "How was your stay there?"

I said only, "That was not the job for me." And I left it at that.

Visiting the Avenue

The Cary Home would let us see our parents once every month. They had to say it was OK with my mother and step dad. I could see them only on the second Sunday of the month, from 12:00 to 5:00 p.m. This was because I was going to church on Sundays, and a church bus would pick me up at the Cary Home. On the second Sunday, I would go down to the Avenue to see my mother, and before five o'clock they would take me back to the Cary Home.

Sometimes my mother wasn't home on the second Sunday, and I would go over to Paul's house. He was a friend of mine, and when it was time to go back to the Cary Home. I would walk back to the Cary Home, and arrive around five o'clock.

What was the Avenue? It was not one of the best places to live, if someone asked you where you lived. But, I must say, that I had a lot of very good friends that lived down on the Avenue.

It was about one mile long, three blocks wide; the neighbors made it their business to know the people that lived in their neighborhood. Up and down the Avenue, from one end to the other end, it was considered one of the lowest places in town to live.

When I would graduate from Jefferson High School, I would move in with my mom and my stepdad. My brother, Joe, had been living there for two years before me. The people on the Avenue treated me like I had lived there all of my life. They knew my name and where I lived, and my mother and stepfather.

You may wonder where they got a job or who they worked for. A large number of the men worked for the City. My stepdad worked for the City Water Works. This is how the lowest class was being taken care of by the upper class. These are the kind of people Christ liked to walk with, when he walked the earth.

Some of the people that lived on the Avenue, where my new life would be starting, where like Flower that lived in the desert of sin, and were very happy with their way of life.

When it was time for me to go back to the Cary Home, Mom and Jim loaded me up in the old black Buick, the best car that was ever made. That's the way my stepdad Jim saw it!

When we would arrive at the Home, I would get out and say, "Thanks for the ride," and they left. This was the only time that we could go in the front doors, and let them know I was back.

Last Day in the Cary Home

My shop teacher, Mr. Leavitt, would let me into all the basketball games. He knew I didn't have any money to pay to get in, and as long as they were home games, it would be free for me and my friend Paul.

Mr. Leavitt always treated me kindly. My last day in school, Mr. Leavitt came up to me, saying he had some good news for me. That he found me a job working at the high school for the summer. He said that if they liked my work, they would keep me permanently.

Now it was Saturday, time for my step dad Jim and my mom to pick me up, out in front of the Cary Home. As I was getting ready to leave the Cary Home for Children for the last time, I was headed out the front door.

Larry Knox came and said for me to hold out my hand. He dropped my allowance into it. He said, "It's yours, you worked for it." I looked down to see what it was, thirty-five cents. He said, "You might need it." I said, "Thanks and goodbye."

Larry said, "Goodbye and good luck."

I headed to the front door. When I came to the Cary Home, I didn't need to sign in. Now that I was leaving, I didn't need to sign out.

As I was standing out in front, I turned and looked at all the windows I saw on the first day I came to the Cary Home, when I was six years old. No more cleaning all the Windows that I and the other boys would clean, year after year.

This was the final end of my old life, and the winds of time were blowing me into an unknown life that was waiting for me.

I came with a sack of clothes and I left with a sack of clothes, and I did gain a pair of dress shoes. Down the driveway was coming the old black Buick, at this time in my life, it was the best car ever made coming to pick me up. I was going to stay with my mother and stepdad, and my brother Joe, on 922 Queen Street, one block east of the "Avenue."

As I was getting into the car, I said good morning and told them about the job I got at the high school. I could tell that my stepdad was very happy. He thought maybe I was going to be lazy and lie around like Joe did when he first came and moved in to live with them.

I graduated from Jefferson High School. My mother and sister came to my graduation services. Then I went home with my mother to her house to stay there until the time for the winds of time to blow me in some other direction.

After a week, my stepdad, Jim, said that he had found me an old car to drive to work. I would need to pick it up on Sunday. I could pay him back when I got paid from the school. I did pay Jim back, and thanked him for his help in finding me a car.

On Sunday, Joe, his friend Johnny, and my stepdad Jim, took us to pick up the car. It was on the north end of town. The owner was standing by the car when we pulled up next to the car. He handed over the keys to Jim for a four door mint green Plymouth.

Jim turned and handed the keys to me, and I turned and was going to hand them to Joe.

He said, "It's not my car. It's your car. You drive it home."

But the only car I ever drove was an automatic, not a stick. Then I looked around, and Jim was gone. I looked at Johnny. "Don't look at me," he said. "I don't have legs that work." He was right, when he was very young; he came down with polio in his legs.

I got behind the driver's wheel and put the key in, and tried to start it, but it wouldn't do anything. I looked at Joe and he told me the button to the starter was on the floor. "Step on it." I did and the car jumped forewords, and stopped dead.

Joe said, "You need to push in on the clutch, put it in first gear, and hold the break down when you start it." Very slowly I let out on the clutch, and at the same time pushed on the gas pedal. I did as he said, but it died on me. "Give it more gas," Joe said. The next time I give it more gas, and the down the road we went. "Push in on the clutch." As I did, Joe shifted it into second gear. "Leave it there." Everything was going fine, until we came to town and the lights were turning red and I had to stop.

I put it into first gear and held the clutch in, waiting for the light to change. I had my foot on the brake, and part of the foot on the gas pedal, then the light turned green. I stepped on the gas and let the clutch pedal up.

The car rolled six feet, to the middle of the intersection, and came to a dead stop. I set everything as before, popped the clutch and the car stopped dead. Here we were in the intersection and the light changed to red, and the other cars were laying on their horns! They had to go around us. I looked over at Joe and Johnny. They had slid off their seats and were hiding on the floor. I was a little mad, what kind of help was this?

This time I set everything up again, and when the light turned green, I stepped on the gas pedal and pealed out of there. I was going to make it through the other lights, and I didn't stop until I pulled into the driveway. They got out laughing like it was fun, and I said, "Don't ask for any rides."

It was an old car, when you would turn a corner, it would bank like an airplane. The shocks were gone. If you hit a big bump in the road, it would bounce up and down, until it smoothed itself out or you hit another bump, then it would start all over again. It felt like there was a person bouncing my car like it was a basketball. To stop it from happening I would slow way down before I ran over another bump in the road.

One day I was out in the country. The roads were gravel. I looked into my rearview mirror. The car was kicking up a lot of dust. The next thing I knew it was on the inside of my car. The car was full of dust. I slowed way down and rolled down my windows to let the dust out of the car. When I got back home to my house, I jumped out and picked up the floor mats, and there were holes in the floors, front and back. No more country roads and dust baths for me.

Monday I was standing in front of the high school, looking at my first real job.

At the end of the summer my time was up. I would need to find a new job. The superintendent came up to me and said, Monday, I would be going out to Edgelea School, out on south Eighteenth Street, to start working with Charlie. He would set up my time and show me what I needed to do.

On Monday I went into Edgelea School to see Charlie. He was a lot older, but very nice to me. Charlie said that I would start working at twelve noon until 8:00 p.m., five days a week. And in the summer when the school was out for the summer, we would start at 8:00 a.m. to 5:00 p.m. five days a week. We had six halls and a gym to clean up, and the dirt marks on the walls. You would think I was still in the Cary Home. The work was the same.

After I got off work and went home to supper and clean up, I would walk over to The Avenue. From my house it was only one half block to The Avenue, where Paul and some of the younger kids my age, would hang out, talk, and joke.

One of the girls that was in the group on The Avenue came up to me and said that there was a girl who would like to meet me and talk to me. She said, "Tomorrow night about this time."

I said, "OK, I will be here."

The next night I was sitting and talking to some of the other boys, the girl from the night before came up to me with Cindy. She said, "Here she is." We talked for about thirty minutes and when she was leaving to go home, she said that her mother would like to meet me tomorrow night, before we could go out on a date.

She gave me the address on Queen Street. I knocked on the door, and Cindy came to the door and let me in and introduced me to her mother and father and her sister. I talked to them for some time, about my life at the Carry Home, and my overall plans and where I was working.

I started going with Cindy, and dating her. Over time we were engaged, but she didn't like any of my friends or their girlfriends, or like me to be around them.

I worked there at the school for about three years. I showed Cindy my notice from Uncle Sam that said I was to meet a bus downtown, Maine and Sixth Street, Monday morning, to be taken to Indianapolis for a check up. This was to see if I was eligible for draft, and if I passed the exams, I would be drafted into the army for two years.

Cindy's mother wanted us to get married before I went into the army. I said, "No, I think she should get her education first." We did get engaged, and I went off to the army, December 4, 1963. My boot camp was at Fort Knox, Kentucky. After Fort Knox I was stationed at Fort Sill, Oklahoma.

I came home for Christmas for two weeks, and then back to Fort Knox. After basic training I was sent out to Fort Sill, working in the ammo dump. After that I got a job as the company artist, painting pictures. They would come with the picture that they wanted painted.

I didn't spend all my money in town on loose women and beer. When most of the men came back from town, they would be broke, then I would loan them the money to buy their toiletries at the post exchange. Usually I wouldn't loan any more than ten to fifteen dollars to any one person. I did have one person to whom I'd loan twenty dollars: Smith. When some of them men complained, I would tell them that he was the only one that would come and find me to repay me, but you, I would have to hunt you down to get you to pay me.

I was a coin collector, when I was a civilian. I spent a lot of time looking for coins with an "S" mint mark on them, and I found more of them when I was in the army out West, since all of them were made in San Francisco, on the West Coast.

One day I was walking across the parking lot. I backed up after I stepped off the curb. There was something sticking out of the ground, so I pulled out my pocket knife, and dug it up. It was an old dime, dated 1916, in good shape. How did that coin end up there just waiting for me to come along and find it? What luck!

Six months before I was to get out of the army, the 661st HQ was to ship out to Vietnam. We packed all of our gear in a duffel bag, ready to leave the next morning. When we fell out for roll call, they called my name, told me to fall out and report inside to the captain. He told me to unpack my duffel bag; so I wouldn't be going with them.

The next day I had another captain in charge of me. I was told that I would be going with a new unit that was being set up. The time came for me to pack my duffel bag and get ready to ship out again. I lined up for roll call and got ready to load up on the trucks, and then the captain told me to fall out, and report to battalion headquarters.

I went over to battalion headquarters to the Office of Personnel, and they gave me a room where I was to stay. That's when I found out that I wasn't going to Vietnam, but I would be stationed at Battalion Headquarters, until my time was up in the army. And then I would be discharged from the service.

I don't know how all this came about, some of the men in the six-sixty first had less time than me, with only two or three months to go. They were mad at me because they were going and I was staying. I had six months to go. In the mean time I wasn't getting any letters from Cindy. I knew something wasn't right, but there wasn't anything I could do until I was discharged from the service.

Moving On

When I graduated from high school, I worked for the high school until I was drafted into the army, for two years. When I left for the army, I had a girlfriend named Cindy. In the long run, she had found another boy, and ran away with that person, just as I was being discharged from the army.

I went down to see my ex-girlfriend's parents, Beulah and Orville Thayer. They were the reason that I had a place to stay. They asked me if I had a place to stay I said, "No." So they said that I could stay with them for a while, until I found a good job. Out of gratitude, I helped around the house: mowing the grass, cleaning up the leaves, etc.

Why I didn't stay at my mother's and step father's house, was that my brother Jim got out of the navy and was staying with them; there was no room for me.

My brother, Lynn, called me to see if I still needed or wanted to work with him at the TV and Appliance Store at Market Square Mall. I said, "Sure!" He said I should come down to Market Square on the following Monday, to see about getting the job.

Monday came, and I went down to TV Clinic at 8:00 a.m., and started working for Lou Dunlavey. Together with Lynn, I was delivering TVs, refrigerators, washers, and dryers. We worked from Monday to Friday and sometimes on Saturday.

While I was staying with the Thayers, I ended up getting a new car. This was because when I went into the army, I had to get rid of my old car, a black Oldsmobile convertible with power windows and seats! Now I had no way of getting to work. The new car was a used car; it was a yellow hardtop, four-door sedan.

I would go down to Pop's Filling Station, to see if anyone was trying to get up a basketball game. There was a man sitting on his bike. I walked over to him and asked, "What is your name?" He replied, "Eddie." He had a body like a sixteen year old boy. He was built like a body builder, very strong and muscular. He had a mind and voice of a five year old.

I said, "Come on into the gas station and I'll buy you a Coke." He said, "No." I went on in and paid for a Coke and went outside to give it to him. He took it, but didn't say thanks, and rode his bike on down the road.

Usually, I was at Pop's Filling Station, to see if anyone was trying to get up a basketball game on Saturday, and sometimes on Sunday afternoon. We didn't have a basketball; we would walk over to Donnie's house to see if we could get Donnie's basketball at his house, across the avenue from Pop's Filling Station where his mother lived. Most of the time Donnie wasn't home. He would be working at his mother's grocery store.

His mother would let us use his basketball, and as we were playing the game, Donny would come walking down to the park courts. We would ask him which team he would like to play on. He would hold out his arms so we would pass it to him, then he would turn and walk back home with it and say, "Don't ask for it again." We would say, "Who are you going to play with?" Donny said, "No one, and for sure not you." End of game.

In the winner time we would play on the church team, down at the YMCA and go to church on Sunday. Then we started a soft ball team in the summertime and played on the week days, and on the weekends. We also played in tournaments.

Five of us joined a bowling league in the wintertime: Tuesdays and Thursdays. The Thursday team was a no handicap; there were a lot of good players in it.

I was doing all of this before I met my wife, Melanie. I stopped in to get gas at Pop's. Eddie must have seen me, and when I came out to leave, there was Eddie sitting on his bike.

I said, "Hi, would you like a Coke?" He replied, "Sure." I went back into Pop's and got Eddie a Coke. Then I asked Pop, "Why won't Eddie come into the station?" Pop said, "Because most of the boys that you play ball with make fun of him when he comes around, because he is a little off and slow of mind."

I said, "I see." I went outside, and I handed Eddie the Coke. I saw a black lunch bucket wired to his handlebars on his bike.

I pointed at the black lunch bucket. I asked, "Do you carry your tools in it to fix your bike?"

Eddie said, "It's my lunch."

I said, "What do you have in your lunch bucket?

He reached down and opened it up so I could look in, and there was only a large can of pork and beans and a spoon in it.

"Do you have a job?" I asked.

He responded by saying, "At the American Marietta."

I said, "Isn't that company just down the road? Don't they make cement beams for bridges?" He said, "Yes, one of my jobs is to clean out the mixers." Then he left on his bike, and pedaled on down the road. This would be the last time I would ever see

Eddie alive. Two days later, one of the workers where he worked, thought it would be funny to turn on the mixer, when he was inside of it trying to clean it out.

He was dead before he knew what hit him. This is why you should be kind to every one you meet. You never know what's waiting for you or them down the road.

When I needed gas for my car, I would stop in and get my gas from Pop's Station. As I was standing outside waiting for the car to fill up, I would look over and in my mind's eye, I would see Eddie sitting there on his bike, one foot on the ground and the other one on one of the pedals. He would be looking at me. Tied to the front handlebars was the black lunchbox, with a can of pork and beans inside of it. Eddie was gone for good.

"And it shall come to pass afterwards that I will pour out my spirit on all flesh. Your sons and your daughters shall prophecy, your old men shall see visions."

—Joel 2:28-32

Out of the Cary home
there will be a new
light in my life.

Working at TV Clinic

I was working at TV Clinic at the Market Square Mall for about two years, with my brother Lynn. I started out as a helper and as a delivery man, with my brother Lynn at the TV Clinic. The owner, Lou, came up to me to see if I would like to go to school, in Indianapolis to learn how to repair televisions. After a year I would repair the TVs in the homes of the customers, and also in the repair shop, with three other service men.

On Tuesdays and Thursdays, I would go to class from 6:00–9:00 PM. This lasted for one year. Fred was the one who would go out and make in-home repairs, and after six months I started going out with him. In time I would take over the outside service calls.

One of the other jobs I had was to climb up on the houses. The only way you could watch TV programs was through the air and to your TV's antenna outside your home. I would repair the TV antennas, or put up new ones, and also climb the antenna towers. We worked on microwaves and VCRs also.

When I first started out on service calls, I had a tool box, and two suitcases that were full of tubes for the TVs.

Over time we moved from Market Square to Tri-Angle Enterprise. It was located out on north 52 Highway. Then Lou started renting small refrigerators for students at Purdue University, that they could use in their dorm rooms or rented room to hold cold drinks. He would rent them to the Purdue students by the semester. Then we moved to five points, and I still was worked on TVs and antennas.

Then Lou closed the TV repair shop. My brothers Jim and Joe found out that I wasn't working anymore on TVs, and came to get me to help on a new job up in Goodland. I would need to join the construction workers' union.

Now I was in the union, building a school; I worked there for one year, until the job was finished. Then I went back to West Lafayette, to work on a retirement home. I met George, who was a brick layer. He said that he was the pastor of the First Church of God in Frankfort, Indiana.

I came home from work one evening, and Beulah said that Mindy, her granddaughter, had a teacher that I needed to meet. Beulah handed me the telephone number for me to call with her name on it: Melanie Werner. That was all that I knew about her.

On Friday I called her, and set up a time to meet her on Saturday. We met for a Coke to see if she would like to go out on a date, and she said, "Yes!" Our first date was to a dance in Lafayette, I didn't dance, but we went anyhow.

Over time we were going out and I was going to her church in Frankfort on Sundays. And when I went into the church for the first time, there was George, the pastor from work.

"What are you doing here?" Pastor George Denniston asked.

"I came here to go to church with Melanie Werner." I responded. "We're glad to have you," George said.

After a few months, I was given the job of taking up the offering, with Joel and Johnny. Week after week I would stand in the back of the sanctuary and pick up the offering. As I stood there looking at the back of the people's heads, I wondered how God knew who was a believer and who wasn't.

Seeing Lynn

When I left the Cary Home, after graduation from high school, I would go out on Saturdays and see my brother. Lynn Sheets lived on a farm on the west side of Lafayette. The Sheets family changed Lynn's last name to Sheets from Holsclaw. He needed to if he wanted to inherit part of their turkey farm.

We walked all over the farm looking for targets to shoot, trying to outdo one another. Sometimes we would throw rocks into the air, and take turns hitting them, until one of us missed.

One Saturday, Lynn came out of his house, with a hundred-year-old antique long barrel ball and cap rifle. When he brought it, it used flint to fire it off. Sometimes it would fire, sometimes it wouldn't. Sometimes it would fire as you lowered the gun. Lynn didn't like using it that way, never knowing for sure when it would go off.

So he changed it over to a cap. When the hammer would hit the cap, it would fire, every time. He loaded it up with black powder and put a cap on the housing. Lynn cocked it and told me to try it out. I said, "What is there to shoot at?"

He said, "See that old combine about two hundred yards out in the field?"

I said, "Yes; how far up in the air should I aim to hit it?"

Lynn said, "Straight at it." The distance to the target was two hundred yards. From where we were standing in the gravel road. I aimed and pulled the trigger! It made a large cloud of black smoke that filled the air. When the ball hit the metal, there was a loud noise. The sound came from the combine when the lead hit the side of it. We walked over to a look at it. It had a big hole in its side. It was over one hundred yards away.

We were walking back down the driveway to the house. I had told my brother Joe that I was going out to Lynn's house to shoot rifles. Our bother Joe and sister Annette pulled up in the driveway to see what we were doing. We showed them the ball cap rifle.

Lynn said, "Have you ever shot one of these guns, Joe?"

Joe said, "No, but let me try it!"

I said to Lynn, "Load it up, Lynn." He put in the black powder and a lead ball, a piece of old rag cloth to hold it in place, so the lead ball wouldn't work out onto the ground. "Here you are, Joe," Lynn said. Lynn told Joe to aim at the combine out in the field, just aim straight at it, but hold it tight to his arm.

Joe put it to his arm. When he pulled the trigger, a large cloud of black smoke filled the air. It was hard to see the combine for the smoke, but you could hear the noise it made when it hit metal. And at the same time, it knocked Joe to the ground. He jumped up rubbing his arm. Joe said, "Did it knock you to the ground like that, Lynn?"

Lynn said, "Not me, I know how to hold it. Did you have any problems, Bill?"

"Not me, you must have used a full load, where we used only a half load. Maybe our sister Annette (who's birth name was Hazel before she was adopted out when she was two years old) would like to try it?" Annette and Joe turned and started walking to the car. I guess not.

Lynn and I would meet every Saturday and practice on our shooting. We were down along a creek, and we were looking at a tree that was sitting out in the open field. "Wouldn't that make a good tree house?" Lynn said.

I said, "Yes. Why don't you wait until next Saturday, when I come out, I will help you build it." It didn't take long for a week to go by. I was pulling up to the farm and parking my car in front of the farmhouse. He must have been looking for me, as he was standing next to my car before I could get out. Come on down and look at the tree house, it's all built."

We walked down to the field. I could see it off in the distance, sitting up off the ground about fifteen feet in the tree, a ladder going up the tree, to a small porch, going to the front door, and next to the window. Lynn had put in a door, and we walked in. Lynn said, "How does the inside look to you, and what do you think of the tree house?"

"I see you didn't wait for me to help you, but it looks good and strong." As we climbed back down, we were standing there looking it over, I said, "If you wait for me next week, I can help you run a cable from the top of the hill, down to the tree house, and you can come in the front door by air."

Next week I pulled up in the drive and Lynn was standing in front of my car.

"Come and see the tree house now. "We walked down the creek to the tree house, and stopped in front of the tree. Lynn said, "How does it look to you from this side?" I said, "It still looks good to me."

"I see you put up the cable, from the hill down to the tree house."

"Do you see anything else?" Lynn said.

I looked around and everything seemed to be in its place.

Lynn said, "Come around here and look at the back."

I walked to the back side, and looked up, and the back side was blown away. I said, "What happened to the back side?"

Lynn said, "Well I did like you said. I found some cable that was a hundred feet long, enough to go from the top of the hill, down to the creek and across the water to the tree house. When I got to the top, I got a ladder so I could hook the cable up high above the door, I pulled it tight, and left it with a little give in it.

I went to the top of the hill and hooked the pulley to the cable, then I stepped off the log, so I would get a clear start. Down the hill, I was moving very fast, it was working like it should, then I came to the creek, where I should have been starting up to the front door, there was too much slack in it. I ended up in the creek water, face down and all wet.

I went to the top of the tree house, and retied the cable, this time it would work. I picked up the pulley and climbed to the top of the hill, and put the pulley on and jumped up and down to see how tight it was, it was just right.

I stepped on the log, and down the hill, everything was going well. I crossed the creek and didn't touch the water, and I was going up to the door, and I put on the brakes, but the brakes didn't slow me down any. I went through the front door with my feet in front of me, through the inside and out the back of the tree house and onto the ground. I didn't get hurt, but that's how the back of the tree house got knocked out. We forgot one thing: that we would need to stop at the front door!"

As far as I was concerned, I wouldn't be using the hill or the cable, just the ladder. Over time, Mr. Sheets had Lynn take the tree house down, and make it like it was before Lynn came along.

Reading the Bible

I was reading the Bible, and it said that we should meditate, and listen to the word of the Lord (Joshua 1:7–8).

When I would meditate, it would be when I would get ready to go to bed in the evening. I would lie in bed with my arms down to my side, close my eyes, and still my mind. The next thing I knew, it was morning, and it was time for me to get up and go to work.

The next night I would do the same thing, and then it would be morning, I would get up and go to work. I didn't give up on meditating, and soon I was able to hold on, and not go to sleep.

The next night I had a dream. I was in a Doctor's office where he was examining me. The Doctor then said, "I know what the problem is."

"After all the tests I ran on you, I'm finding it hard to believe. But you are pregnant and are going to give birth in two months. This will be the first in the world and I'm so excited! Then I woke up.

I was having a hard time trying to understand what the dream meant to me. Over a week or two I would think what it meant. It didn't mean that I was actually going to give birth to a live baby, but to a new thought, and heading into a world of new thought. In two weeks I was now reading the Bible where it says be quiet and listen to God.

Now I had started meditating on the Bible, the Lord's word. As I lay in bed with my arms down to my side, quieting my mind, the next thing I knew I found myself surrounded by lost souls living in the deepest and the darkest place, where souls go, when they don't have faith or believe. They lived in what we would call a living hell. If you don't find God, and you believe that there is nothing after you die, in the end, that is what you get: nothing!

They had me locked in a circle and told me that they were never going to let me out. I would be with them forever, but I would have to stay with them in the dark, and they would never release me. Now I knew what it felt like to be a butterfly that struggles but can't get out of the spider's web.

Somehow I knew that if only I could just get my eyes open a little bit and see some light, they could not hold me, I could break their spell on me.

So I put all my strength and energy into opening my eyes. Even if I was locked in hell with them, I had a body, in a meditating state, in my bedroom. If only I could wake up my flesh and get it to crack its eyes open. We were still separated; one part of me was in the flesh, in the bedroom, and another part, in hell, when apart. The two parts of my whole being should fuse together. I sent this thought to my body and sure enough, it worked.

When I forced my eyes open again I could see the faint streetlight through the window of my bedroom. I was back in my bed, free from the darkness: my soul was back in my body!

So the next night, I made up my mind that I needed to put Christ in my mind to guide me and protect me. Before I would meditate again, I would pray that the Lord would watch over me when I closed my eyes.

The next time I meditated, I found that I was up in the air above the tree tops. There was a steeple on a building that was giving off multicolored hues of light. There was light to see things, but no sun.

Very slowly I started floating down to the ground, when I came to rest just above the ground; I looked up and saw an archway in the door. Now I knew that the building was a church. It was one of the things that you felt, because it gave you the sense of what it was, without being told that it was a church.

I turned and went down the path that was there and through the trees, up and over and down the low hills. Everything had a synchronous wave rhythm. The trees were vividly green, as was the weed-free grass path that I was floating above the ground on, not walking. Everything was radiantly bright in color! Then I found myself back in my body, and awake.

The next night I was getting ready to meditate, but before I could, I saw a faint light in the corner of the kitchen. I looked to my left, and I saw that the wall that I was lying next to had disappeared, and I was looking through the open wall, into the living room and into the kitchen. Everything was dark, but there was a light coming out of the kitchen corner, and it was moving toward me, I could make out the shape of a figure. The glowing light stayed with the figure only as it moved my way.

I watched as it went through the living room stove, and came over and stood in the opening where the wall used to be. It was next to where I was lying in bed. The angel had a full robe that was brown, and I could also see his hands locked together in the front of the robe. I saw the front of his nose sticking out of the hood.

He was looking down at me; he moved his head up and down, from my head to my stomach, and back up to my head and then back down my body.

He didn't say anything but turned around and moved back through the stove as he moved to the corner of the kitchen. The light went with him as he moved to the far side of the kitchen. When the light went out, he was gone, and the wall was back the way it was before he came. I said to myself, "At least you could have said something to me!"

The more I thought about it, the more I realized he wasn't looking at my flesh, but at my soul. He was looking at my soul, because there are seven spiritual centers (tests) that we must overcome in this world before we can move on.

It was and is the soul that God cares about, not the material world. This is the world where the tests are being handed out to every soul. These tests include keeping God's commandments, loving and forgiving one another, and putting God's service and others needs before your own. You need to be hunting for God's true love. God is the one who made the souls, and it was from his overwhelming love, that He has for us.

It is your turn to make the right choices.

when I was 23 yrs old

Does God See You?

It was a Saturday morning, I was at home and the telephone rang, and I answered it. Paul called to see if I would like to go fishing with him out on County Road 900 South. I said, "Sure." I wasn't doing anything.

Where we wanted to go fishing was called Big Fishing Camp Ground. So I drove over to his house, we loaded up the fishing pole and the bait and headed to the pay pond.

We paid at the office to fish, and headed to the spot that we liked to go when we fished there. I went on the east side of the pond and Paul was on the north side of the pond. It was a very nice day in April. The sun was shining and the weather was warm.

When I looked to see where Paul was, I looked around and saw that Paul was trying to climb on the roots of a tree that was half in the water and half out of the water, in trying to sit so he could cast his line.

I went to my spot and cast my pole out into the middle of the pond, but I didn't put any bait on the hook, I had planned on just lying on the side of the hill, enjoying the warm sun on my face and pondering God.

I had just picked up a stick and I was bouncing it up and down on the ground. I was thinking a lot about God and how he had worked in my life. I thought to myself, "God! Do you know me? God! Do you see me? God! Do you hear me? And if you do, bring the biggest fish in this pond to the surface where I cast my line in the center of the pond, so I can see it. And I will know you know me."

As I lay there on my side, balancing the stick up and down on the ground, now and then I would look out across the water to see if I could see a fish at the surface of the pond, and then I would look back at my stick, bouncing it up and down on the ground again and looking up at the water to see if there was a fish, and I would bounce the stick up and down again and again after five or six times.

I could feel some one behind me, that was looking at me from my back, and when I looked over my shoulder, down at the edge of the bank, was a very large fish halfway out of the water, just resting on a log that was at the edge of the bank.

I looked at it, and it looked back at me. It was not breathing hard or grasping for air. After thirty seconds or so, the fish backed off very slowly from the log, and moved out into the pond about ten feet from the bank, and then came out of the water, so I could see how big it was. Now I knew that God sees me, knows me, hears me.

Now I walk through life knowing that He is with me and you in our lives. That God knows you, God sees you, God hears you. God wants to be part of your life and God wants you to be part of God's life.

Ask, seek, and wait. God knows you, God hears you, and best of all, God sees you.

Hunting out West

Before I met my wife Melanie, I was going out west in the fall with my ex-girlfriend's brother, Gary, and his friends, deer hunting in Wyoming.

One of the men in our group, knew of a ranch. Two hired hands, John and Lee were taking care of the ranch over the winter months, until spring came. Then they would take care of the cattle.

They invited Gary Thayer, and four other friends that he wanted to take with him, to hunt on Elk Mountain. We would have to bring a trailer, because we couldn't sleep in the bunk house or have our meals there. It was shut down for the winter, and there was no heat. We could stay at the ranch, at no cost to us. John and Lee would be our guides up in the mountains, and show us the best places to hunt.

We started out in the middle of November. We had put all of our equipment in the trailer, with the food in back of the truck. We loaded up and headed out to Wyoming. The ranch itself is set at the base of Elk Mountain.

On the way out of Indiana, we had a bad tire on the back of the truck. So we stopped in Indiana, and we had to buy a new tire for the truck.

We all chipped in to pay for the tire and have it put on the back of the truck. Our plans were to drive through the night, and get to the ranch in the morning.

But as we were traveling the weather got very cold. I was sleeping in the back of the truck, and my feet were getting numb with cold, that was what woke me up. To warm them up, I tried to wiggle them, but after some time, I was not having any luck with that. My feet were still hurting, so I said to myself "Oh, my God! Help me!" No sooner had the words come out of my mouth, there was a loud bang, and the truck pulled over to the side of the road. I got out of the back very carefully and walked slowly up to the front of the truck because my feet were stinging.

I climbed up into the truck, and as I was waiting in the front seat, I put my feet in front of the heater to warm them up. Gary and the driver, "Tiny," climbed back in and opened the front door. I said that I wasn't going to ride in back, because my feet were too cold. Then one of the other guys riding up in front said that he would ride in the back of the truck, because he was tired.

As I was sitting in front, and my feet were warming up, I asked.

"What was the problem with the truck?" Gary explained that they had to replace the new tire, because it had a blowout. They could not understand how that could have happened. I never told them that I had called on the Lord to help me, and that he had heard me and came to my rescue, in my hour of need!

To this day they aren't any wiser about what happened on that dark lonely road going out West, but I knew that the Lord was with me!

Our Old New House

When I first saw my wife to be, I saw her in a dream, standing there in the dawn of darkness. She was looking around to the right and left, as if she was waiting for time to catch up to her and me. The image of her was in the dawn of morning.

After two years later I met her, and we were married. I moved to Frankfort, Indiana. We lived in an apartment, on the second floor.

With help from her parents, we found a house over on First Street in in Frankfort, Indiana. It was new to us. The first thing we did was to fix it up the way we wanted it, putting in a patio, and a wall in front with a side walk.

One day as I was working in the back yard, I noticed something looking at me, but when I looked to see what it was, it was gone. Just the swaying of the rocking chair was evidence that something had been there. After three or four times of this I stopped working, walked over to the chair and moved it out of the way.

There lying on the patio was a little kitten, looking up at me. I went into the house, and came out with some food for it. From that time on we had a friend, who would be waiting for us to come out in the morning. She would be there when we came home, after we got off work.

In 1978, in the wintertime, we had big ice storm that dumped about an inch of ice on us. I put on my ice skates, skated up and down First Street. Winter came, and it turned cold outside, so we let the kitten live in the house with us.

One Saturday morning we were going to sleep in, but as I lay there on my side, facing the open door to the living room, I saw the kitten crouching in the door, ready to run into the kitchen. The cat said to me, "Bill, feed me. Feed me, Bill." And then I opened my eyes, the kitten was in the door, just as I saw her, but my eyes were closed. The kitten talked to me with her thoughts, not with her voice.

I saw "Sniffy" with my soul eyes, and not with my flesh eyes. Then it hit me that we all have souls, and 99 percent of the time we are not aware of it.

You never know when God will work in your life, and how He will show you a gift from Him to you. And what a gift it is! You are part of Him, and now you need to show Him the love He shows you.

In a Roman Village

In this dream I was standing up on a hill that looked down over a village. It was back in the Roman times. People were living more like animals than human beings.

They had open waste in their gutters and in the roads. Children were playing in the water and mud. Then I said to them, "Take me to your king." When I stood in front of the king, I said, "I can help improve your standard of living, by cleaning up the town and the peoples' living habits." And before I knew it, they were running me out of town.

I saw myself standing back up on the hill, with tears running down my cheeks, looking down on the village, and I said, "I only wanted to help them to have a better life."

Then a voice came out of the sky, saying, "Bill, some people just don't want any help; they are happy with the way things are."

There are times in your life when you can't seem to help some people. You know and see it in some of the people that live close to you. When you reach out to help them out of a problem, the next thing you know they're back in the same fix or another problem that is worse. There is just no light at the end of the tunnel for them.

I'm not saying that we should give up on them. In these cases, you wonder who is getting the real lesson.

Walking with Jesus

I had a dream where I was walking with Jesus in the desert. There were men and women walking behind us. We were moving at a very fast pace across the desert, we were trying to talk, but these people would not let us talk. That was why we were walking very fast; we were trying to get away from them.

But they were shouting curse words and using God's name in vain. I stopped and turned to them, and said, "Don't you know that if God wanted to, He could make you disappear just like that?" I snapped my fingers at them.

We turned and started walking again. Then we came to the edge of the cliff. The people behind us came to a complete stop, but we walked right up into the sky.

When I turned to look at the people, I saw them standing at the edge, with their arms up in the air and their fists waving at us. Then a voice came out of the sky and said to me, "Bill! God is love."

Tina Calls for Help

I was home one evening, during the wintertime, and I received a telephone call from my niece. She said, "Uncle Bill, do you know what I want?"

I was just about to say no, but in my mind's eye, I was looking down into a deep well. It was twenty feet deep. The water came up to about two feet from the top of the well, and the form was in a circle, like a wishing well. The walls of the well were made out of rocks. The water itself was crystal clear all the way to the bottom.

I saw at the very bottom, a bubble moving up toward me. As it came up, it moved back and forth, as if it was doing a dance and couldn't wait to get to the top of the well. When it was at the very top, it burst and the bubble said, "She wants to go ice skating."

And I said to Tina, "You would like me to take you ice skating, over at the Colombia Park pond, in Lafayette."

And she wanted to know how I knew, she wanted me to-take her ice skating at the park. I told her I saw it in my mind's eye. We left it at that.

The reason I'm putting this short story in these writings is, it shows God can and will work with you in your life. It can happen unexpectedly, and you don't know when or why. This is how some of the things come to me, in unusual ways. You can never know how God will work in your life.

This shows me how God can work in my life, and let you know that He knows you, and He sees you. And He hears you.

He wants to be part of your life and help you with what is going on in your life. So let your door always be left open for the Lord.

Ask, seek, and wait. He knows you, He hears you, and He sees you.

Cell Phone from God

This is a story I had one night: it was a dream, and I found myself walking into a kitchen. It was one I had never seen before. It was very bright and well lit, and there was a person standing on the far side of the table. There was a person sitting at the kitchen table, on the far side from where I was standing. This person said, "Sit down, Bill, I want to show you something."

As I was sitting down, I noticed that he had something in his hand; it looked like the color of gold to me, and a white button in the middle of its face. As I looked at it, he said to me, "This is all you need to reach God. You see what I have in my hand, it is like a cell phone, but it has one button, and when you want to reach God, you just hit the white button, and he will hear what you want or pray for. And the batteries, well, they never run down."

This tells us that God had the first cell phone from the beginning of time! Too bad that more people don't get on God's plan. The plan has unlimited data, and you can call from anywhere. It works day or night.

The best part is the plan is free.

Golden Gloves of Trustworthiness

I think the reason I had this dream was from a conversation in the church. Some people thought that God would punish His children. I told them that God was a God of love; not a God of pain. It is the sins of the people that cause the consequences of pain and suffering.

One of the things you need to see is what kind of God you would like to serve. I was sticking up for God. This dream was God's way of showing me He approved.

In this dream, I'm sitting at a dining room table, which could seat eight people. The room is very bright, it has a golden haze in the air, and to my right is a little old woman at the head of the table, with short gray hair and a flowered dress on. There is a little girl standing next to her right side.

I looked to my left when I heard thunder. There was a window that I could see out, and a storm was coming off in the distance, with lighting and thunder, and the wind was blowing. To the right of the window was a room with light shining out the door, but at this time I couldn't see anything in the room.

There is a front room off the dining room. I could hear people running back and forth, yelling, "The end is coming, God is going to condemn us all to hell!"

I looked out the window and saw that the storm was much closer. I then looked back at the old woman who was looking at me very intensely, and the child next to her started crying. The people in the front room were saying that the Lord was near. We needed to hide because judgment day was here.

I looked back out the window, and the storm was right outside of the house. Now it was very dark and raining and the lighting was very loud and bright.

I turned and looked at the little old lady who was half way out of her chair, leaning over the table, looking at me very intensely, and I said, "That is not God. God is love." As she rose up she said, "You are right," and she turned into an angel and was flying above the table, and said, "You are now given the golden gloves of trustworthiness." And I looked down and the gloves were on my hands. Then I looked to my left out the window and saw, the wind was not blowing, lighting and thunder were gone, the sun was shining, the sky was blue.

When I looked back at the angel, she was gone. I got up and went into the next room where there was a place to put the golden gloves on a stand that was made for them. There was a light shining down on them. Then I woke up.

What the dream meant to me is I was being tested. To see how I would react to the scene that was laid out before me. Then I was given the golden gloves, showing that I passed the test.

What was the test? That God is a God of love, not fear and pain, but a God that wants to live in our lives, and be a part of us, as a caring father would be, caring, giving. Like a mother watching over her children. Don't blame God for all of your problems. He is the answer to your entire situation in your life.

Lampstand

Before I was married to my wife, Melanie, she lived in Frankfort, Indiana. I lived in Lafayette, Indiana.

We attended the First Church of God in Frankfort, Indiana. I was one of the ushers that would help pick up the offering, and take it downstairs and count it with Johnny, the church treasurer. As I stood in the back of the church, week after week, I would only see the backs of the people's heads.

And I would think to myself, "How does God know who is a Christian and who isn't a Christian?" That night as I went to bed, unbeknownst to me, I would find out in a dream. God would show me.

In a dream I found myself going into the First Church of God, and up the steps to the top of the landing. When I looked up at the sanctuary, I was surprised to see that all of the items were gone: no piano, no organ, the pulpit, chairs, everything was completely gone.

But there was standing in the middle of the floor, a lampstand with a lampshade on it. I went to the front of the sanctuary to find out what had happened to all of the items. They should have been where they belonged.

As I started up the aisle, I got about halfway to the front. A voice came out of the air. "Bill, this is how God can tell who is a Christian, and who is not a Christian. The lampstand is the person, the shade is the face, the stand is the body, the base is their feet, the light bulb is the head, and if your cord is plugged into the source, your light is on."

"Some people don't plug into the source, and some people turn their switch on and off. The sad part is that some people have lost their plug."

This is how God knows who is plugged into Him and who is not. If you love God you will leave your light on all the time. He does.

Truck Stuck in the Snow

In late February, I was getting out of bed to go to work, and I saw that it had snowed.

So I got dressed, had something to eat, and headed out the door to my van. The snow that was on the ground was about six inches deep. I stopped at the gas station. I paid for gas and a cup of coffee and headed out on State Road 28 west, to I-65 north.

As I approached I-65 north, I noticed that the semis and cars were going very slowly, but state Road 28 had been treated with salt. It was wet from the snow that had melted on the road, but the road was in pretty good shape for traveling.

I could see that I-65 had a glare of ice on it, and some of the cars were in the ditch. So I went over I-65, staying on State Road 28, but the traffic was very slow.

When I came to a town called Fickle, there was a country road that went straight ahead. I decided that I would take the country road to State Road 52 north.

The reason that I chose it was because I saw that someone had taken their vehicle down that road. They had made a trail so that my truck could ride on their tire tracks to the highway.

So I was feeling pretty good about myself. I finally got out of the traffic that was moving too slow for me!

I made a choice to go down the country road; it was a one lane gravel road, covered with snow. So I'm going down the country road, everything was nice, but whoever was driving the vehicle before me, decided to make a donut hole half way down and in the middle of the road.

I tried to keep my truck in the tracks to get to the far side and back on the trail, but my truck slid off the trail that was now a part of the donut hole. I was trying to keep it moving forward in the snow, but the snow was too deep. I would only slide and stop, so I put it in reverse, went backwards, and forward. The truck would move a little at a time, until it wouldn't move at all.

Then I opened the door to get out, and I saw how deep the snow was and it was drifting up over the threshold of the door, so I stepped in the snow to get to the front of the truck.

The only way I had to move the snow was to use my foot to get as much of the snow away from my tires. I did the same to the back tires. This way I was trying to make a path so I could move my tires, and maybe I could get the truck so it would move at least back and forth. If only I could get my truck to line up on the tracks of the previous vehicle. But all this effort was to no avail.

I was stuck in the snow and nowhere to go, no houses around, no one to come out here, to help me get out of this predicament!

I shut the truck off, and I prayed to the Lord, "You can see that I am in a helpless situation, and I need you to put your hand on the back of the truck, and give me a shove to get back onto the tracks. I trust you will hear me, and you will help me, and now I'm going to start the truck up and put it in gear."

I started the truck up and put it in gear. I stepped on the gas, and it was like my truck flew out of the snow and onto the trail! I said, "Thank You Lord, Thank You!" And down the road I went to State Road 52 north.

When I came to the State Road 52, the road was at a forty-five-degree angle to the highway, so I turned the steering wheel, but the tires would not turn, and I put on the brakes, and backed up to the country road, and I turned my wheels back and forth, but they did not want to turn. They did move a little, and so I was able to go forwards and backwards. So little by little I got some of the packed snow out of the wheels, and finally was able to get my truck in line with the highway.

So I headed to Lafayette, and when I looked down at my gauges, I saw that the generator was not working, so I headed to Parker's filling station. Parker's filling station was one block over from 52 on South Street, but I had to make a very hard left turn to get my truck to make the turn on South Street, then over to Earl Avenue. Parker's sat right on the Corner, but the garage doors were on the north side of the building. I drove through the Mar-Jean Mall that took me through the parking lot and across Earl Avenue to the garage doors, to Parker's station to get my truck repaired.

I went inside and said my generator was not charging on my truck. Bill, the owner, said that he and Jerry would take a look at it. Jerry jumped in the van and had a very hard time trying to get it to line up on the lift. They wanted to get it up in the air so they could look at it from the bottom, but the bottom was full of packed snow. He jumped out and lifted the hood and looked inside, but the only thing he could see from the top was snow. It was packed in the motor and the generator. That was the reason why the generator had shorted out. When I looked in the hood it was hard to believe how bad it was! You would have needed to see it in person. All the wheel wells were filled with snow. So Bill told me to come back and get the van in about six hours, after all the snow had melted off it.

I stopped in around noon to see if it was done, and Bill said that it was still melting, but they could put the generator on, and knocked off the snow in the wheel wells. I climbed into the truck and went to work.

To have God on your side is the best thing you can do and to love God as much as He loves you.

A Lot of Money in My Hands

This is a dream that I had in the year of 1991. I was by myself in this dream, standing outside and it was during the daytime. I'm standing in front of a tree, and in the background is a house to my right side, the sun was shining, and it was warm, the grass is green, and the sky was blue.

As I looked at myself standing there, I noticed that I was holding money in my hands. I had two pockets on my short sleeved shirt, and my front pants pockets were all filled with money. It wasn't small money, it was twenties, and some of the smaller money would fall to the ground, and I didn't care.

Then I woke up from the dream, and I thought to myself, I will never get this much money. Two weeks later, February 1991, we had an ice storm that knocked off all of the branches. Every tree in our area lost its branches, and our electrical power was also knocked out for weeks.

The odd thing about this dream was that I had it two weeks before the storms ever happened, how one could know what the weather was going to be, and then the Lord put it in a form of a dream. He showed me that God is in charge of the weather, and knows what is taking place on the earth.

But yet it happened, and I think about this sometimes. And now I know that the weather is also controlled by the Lord. He must see everything that is going to happen in this world, before it happens and is known, and can be predicted ahead of time.

And why was I holding so much money in my hands, shirt pockets, and pants pockets? Because I worked on antennas and towers. This was before there were ever any cable companies. This was how people would watch television, no cable bills, just pulled it out of the air. When the ice storm came, it covered the antenna with ice on the arms, and the weight of the ice was too heavy. It would break off the arms on the main antenna mast. No signal meant no picture on the TV, which meant lots of repair business for me

God is in charge of the weather also. Give thanks to God.

Ball Silicon Stretchy String

When Lou closed his TV repair center, I worked with my brothers, Jim and Joe; then joined the Hod Carriers Union. I had been in the union for about three years, when I found there was a TV Center looking for someone to repair TVs. I was getting tired of working outdoors in the wintertime.

I went to Mar-Jean Square to see about the job. Mike was the owner. I started the next day; Mike would go out on the house calls, and I worked in the shop with his mother, who answered the telephone and set up service calls.

About six months later, Bill from Beeson's came over to see me, asked if I would like to work at Beeson's on their TVs. The only difference was that I would be in business for myself, and I would be doing only their products. I would have my own shop in their building. I told Mike I was leaving in two weeks. I was going to work for Beeson's.

I had to get set up with the companies that Beeson's was selling their product for, RCA and Zenith, GE, Sony, VCRs, televisions and microwaves. Beeson's also sold washers, dryers, refrigerators, freezers, and dish washers. They had a team that worked on the hard products.

I would be working on the soft products and the only things we would be working on was the microwaves, because of the electronics in the panel that operate the unit.

As I worked in the morning and went out on service calls in the afternoon, I was having a hard time trying to keep up with the repairs in the service shop. I needed to find someone to help me. I knew of a person, and his name was Bob. I stopped in where he was working and talked to him, and asked him to think about what we talked about, and I would come back the next day. Before he accepted the offer he wanted to know how much money he would need to come up with to become a partner.

I said, "How soon can you start?"

Bob said, "First I need to talk it over with my wife, and I'll get back to you, in a day or two."

Bob came by to talk to me and see what it looked like in my shop. He wanted to see if I had enough tools and electronic equipment to repair the products. He said that his wife would like to talk to me. I stopped by his house around noon time, when he was home for lunch. I did talk to his wife. Her main question was what it was going to cost them. Bob had the same problem that I was having, trying to do repairs and go on service calls. He didn't like going out on calls.

I said, "Here is the way I see it, Bob. I'll do the service calls and you can work inside all the time. I'll do the antenna work also. The only time I will need you will be to help me with pick-ups on televisions is when they need to come to the shop for repair. As for the cost to be a partner with me: there is no charge, if you start in two weeks. I'll give you half of the business and everything that's in the shop. How does that sound to your wife and you Bob?"

Bob looked at his wife. She moved her head up and down. "I'll see you in two weeks," Bob said. "That sounds good to me," I said. I went back to Beeson's store and told Bill, one of the owners, what had transpired between Bob and me.

I would go out in the afternoon to make service calls, and Bob would stay in the shop. I had a van that I used for a company truck for service calls, and I would drive it home and back to work. I was listening to the radio one day, and they were talking out a man who had made a ball that was made out of rubber. It had little arms all over it. When he sold the toy, it made him a millionaire.

When I heard that, I said to myself, "I need to come up with a toy like that." Then I thought, "No, I need to come up with an object that everyone would need to have, all around the world."

That night I had a dream. I saw myself getting out of bed and going into the bathroom. I looked down and saw that I had two rolls of toilet paper, instead of one, the other one was on top of the first one.

I started working on the design I saw in my dream. It took some time before I got it working. I hung it up on my old toilet paper holder, the one that was screwed to the wall, and soon I was selling them for twenty dollars each. They were user friendly, and my wife named it: "The Piggy-back Toilet Paper Rack." We later changed the name to "Rescue Roller."

They were selling so well I had to get a patent on it. I started making them better, and came out with different kinds, and painted them different colors. I was taking orders at the same time for them.

My wife and I started out selling them to our friends and in the flea markets. Then I developed a new product which dispensed paper towels, which we called: the "Germinator," because it would not pass on family germs like a regular cloth towel, you used paper towels. It would hook on to the towel rack, where your hand towel rack hung on the side of the vanity, take off the hand towel and hook the "Germinator" onto the rod.

If you didn't have rod that held the hand towel, we had an upright holder, which held paper towel. You could stand it on the sink, and tear off a sheet, to dry your hands on, and toss the paper towel in the waste basket. There was one for the kitchen that could be put on the counter, or hung up on the wall.

These products would cut down on transfer of germs from the hand towel, to the next person instead of using the cloth towel, and would cut down on passing colds from one person to the next in the household.

Even with all the work I put into the piggy back toilet paper holders, and trying to sell them; they never were a very big hit. When customers asked me what I was trying to sell, only about five percent thought it was worth buying. The cost was $15 each or $20 for two.

Over time I put them up. They now sit in the basement in a box, and when someone wants one, I pull the one with the style and color they want. The cost is ten dollars.

Tennis Dream

When I started to learn to play tennis, the first thing I did was to take lessons. I wanted to get a better understanding of how the game was played, improve my game, and be more competitive.

After two years, I decided to join a league and play on a team. I started out playing on a team as the number two doubles.

Then Sandor, the owner of the tennis club, would set up leagues, so the teams could play indoors through the winter, and at the end of the season, first place would receive a trophy.

Sander, the owner of the club, hired George to give lessons in the Tennis Club, as number two pro. When I took tennis lessons from him, I could tell that George knew what he was doing, and how to teach the right way. From week to week, I was rapidly improving.

The owner of the club, Sandor, came up to me to see if I would like to play on his team. He wouldn't be playing on the team. He was going to be the captain of the team. This was his way of having eight teams, playing in the league. I moved from number two doubles to number two singles.

At the close of the first tennis season, Buster, the captain of another team, came to me to see if I would like to play on his team. There was an opening on his team; a player was leaving, and they needed a person to play the number one spot. We all played in the same league.

The best part was they had their own sponsor that paid for the team dues. The only catch was we had to let the sponsor's son play the number two spot on the doubles team. That was OK with me.

Now I would be playing the number one single spot and playing the top players in the league. One of the players I had to play was Dave; he was a left hander, a very good player. When it came time for me to play him we would end up having to play a tie breaker. I would run out of energy and get beat. This happened most of the time, or our allotted time would run out.

One night I had a dream that showed me how to improve my energy, How to keep it up to finish the game, and what I needed to do to help me win.

In this dream I was playing tennis against Dave, and it ended in a tie breaker; he won the match. I was walking back to the men's locker room, and there was a boy sitting in the hall way. I had to step over him to go on down the hall. I looked down as I was stepping over him and saw that he had a hose in his mouth.

I asked him, "What are you doing with a hose in your mouth?"

He said that he had to keep it in his mouth until then, and about that time the water started running out of his ears.

I moved on down the hall, and on my left was an open room. A voice called me by my name, "Bill." I looked into the room and saw a person standing at a table with a lamp hanging down over the table, like you would see over a pool table. All I could see was the body and not the face. It was being blocked by a long lamp shade, hanging down from the ceiling.

He said, "Bill, come in here. I would like to show you something." When I walked over to the table, I could see that there was a small car sitting on a track, on the outside of the table. A wire was going from the car up to a hook in the center of the light. He held up his thumb and finger so I could see what he held in his hand.

"Look at this." He held it up in his hand. "This is a protein. Watch what happens when I drop it in the hole in the top of the car." the car moved around the table about half way and came to a stop. Then he held up his hand to show me carbohydrate, and then he dropped it in the hole in the car. It took off and made three trips around the table before it came to a complete stop.

This dream was showing me that I needed more carbohydrates, and to drink water until it runs out of my ears. I did as the dream said, and I ended up winning the games from then on.

Dreams do have a place in your life, and help you to overcome problems in your life.

Helping Our Pastor's Wife

After Pastor George passed away, his wife lived in the house. Our new pastor thought it would be a good idea if we, the church, would help Thelma repair the roof that was leaking. A tree limb had fallen on the back side of the roof.

We set up a Saturday morning to work on the roof. People from the church who wanted to help were to bring their tools: hammers, power saws to cut plywood, and roofing nails. The women were fixing drinks and snacks, and water for the workers up on the roof.

I was running a little late. When I pulled into the driveway, I had to park out in front of the house, by the highway. As I was getting out of the truck to open the tail gate to get to my tools, I turned around to see how many workers we had.

As I stood there looking at people on the roof, I saw a clear bubble encase the whole house. The workers and house were in a glow.

I had never seen anything like this before. I stared at it for the longest time. Then it dawned on me what I was looking at. When you have a group of people working on a project, there is a sincere love for the one that needs help. We were all in one accord.

I told our Pastor Daniel what I saw, and some of the other people in our church. I don't think they understood what I was trying to tell them. Maybe that's why they didn't see what I saw.

Job in Detroit, Michigan

In the summer of 2003, at our home on Clay Street, I received a telephone call from Gil, in Chicago, Illinois. He wanted to know if I was doing anything. I said, "No, I was just working around the house."

He said that he needed someone to go up to Detroit, Michigan, and do some work on the TGI Friday Restaurant. Some of the tiles had fallen off the top face of the restaurant, and needed to be replaced.

First, I would have to go to his Chicago store and pick up the materials to do the job. The job needed to be done by Saturday. I said I could go up Saturday morning and do the work. He said the machine that would lift me to the top of the building would be in the parking lot, because the tile was falling off from the top. The painters, who painted the top section, had pulled them off. There were thirty-five pieces of tile that needed to be replaced and put back on.

Gil said that if I would come up Wednesday, he would have $500, so I could get gas and go up there Saturday morning, he would have the rest of the money for me when the job was finished.

Wednesday came, I got up early, and headed to Chicago, to get the materials that were needed for the job, and picked up the money for the trip to Detroit. Then I returned home to Frankfort, Indiana.

So I was up early Saturday morning, and headed to Michigan. My destination was Utica, Michigan. Utica is on the north side of Detroit, Michigan. By the time I arrived at the TGI Friday, it was 10:30 a.m.

There in the parking lot was the lift I was to use to get to the top of the building. I worked on the building for six to seven hours. By the time I was done and put the lift back in the parking lot, I was ready to leave. The sun was setting in the west. I put everything that was left over in the back of my truck. As I was walking around in front of my Ram Truck, I looked down at my front tire. I noticed the part of the tire was wearing through on the passenger side of the truck.

So when I got settled into the truck, I said a little prayer to the Lord, asking the Lord to watch over me, and help me to get on the right roads back to Indiana, and home.

I started up the truck and headed west on a maze of highways. It was getting dark, and the sun was setting in the west and in my eyes as I went down the road, I was looking for buildings and things that I could remember as I came into Utica. After a long ride on I-90, I moved over into the left lane to make a left hand turn onto I-69, heading south to State Road 26 West.

After an hour and a half, I came to the exit for State Road 26 west, and turned to go up the off-ramp. My headlights did not seem to be as bright as they should be. I looked down at my gauges on my front control panel; the generator was not making energy for the battery. My truck was running only from the battery and I knew the battery would be dead soon.

I pulled off to the side of the road. Then I tried to tap on the alternator with the hammer I retrieved from the back of the truck, in hopes that it would loosen the brushes and restart the generator working. My efforts failed. Finally, I turned off all the power to the control panel, the heater, and headlights, and tried to drive in the dark, the compass and temperature lights were the only lights that were on. They glowed a soft red.

I drove down the road, with no headlights on, looking off into the west, hoping to see some lights from the town of Kokomo, Indiana. But the only thing I saw was darkness, and, when I would meet a car that was coming down the other side of the load, I would turn on my headlights for a moment, and when they passed, I would turn my headlights off again.

One of the things that was working for me was that there was a full moon shining. I could see the road very well and some of the things that were on the side of the road. Plus I could see the stop signs as I came upon them. There was only a handful of houses along the road, some with porch lights on, most of them in the dark.

I called my wife up on my cell phone, and let her know what kind of problems I was having coming home. This was around ten in the evening. I told her that I would let her know what was going on, and that she might have to come and pick me up. But for right now, I was going to try to get the truck home, or to Kokomo. So I said goodbye to her and drove on down the road.

As time went on, passing only a few other cars that were coming the other way, my lights were getting dimmer and dimmer. I was hoping that I would come to a small town to get some help to replace my generator, but as it turned out, there were only houses.

I don't know how far I went, but my lights were getting still weaker, so when a car approached me, I would see them, but they would not see my truck. Even the light from the compass and temperature gauge went out. It was just a matter of time, before the truck would come to a complete stop and be dead.

I came to a stop sign, shut the truck off, and said to the Lord, "I am in trouble, and I need your help! You said if I only called on your name, and you would hear me, and come to help me in my hour of need, and as you can see, I need your help. All you have to do is touch the generator, and get the power on.

"I am going to trust that you heard me, and you will come in my time of need, and now I am going to turn the truck on."

So as I turned the key on and the motor roared into life, my headlights were very bright, and I could see everything in front of me. I looked at the panel, and the generator was up and running and charging. You never saw someone so happy, out on a lonely road! I realized I was never by myself, for as long as I had the Lord who hears me, no matter where I am at, He is there also.

I called my wife up and give her the good news, that I would be home soon, that the Lord had heard me when I prayed to Him. She was happy, and I was happier, because I would not be sitting along the dark road, and hoping that she could find me. His much-needed help and His goodness had saved me!

In our life on this earth, what a joy it is to have the Lord on your side!

Waiting for My Help

This story is unusual. Sometimes there are things I don't understand. And I don't know why I see them, but I'll tell it. the way it happened to me.

At the end of the week, for us that was a Friday, my helper told me to pick him up on Monday, and I said to him, "I'll be there to pick you up." I needed him ready to go when I'd get there, because we had a lot of ceramic tile to lay down on Monday. He said that wouldn't be any problem. He would be up and ready to go, and in the back of my mind, I said to myself, "I don't think he will be up and ready to go." But I needed his help just the same.

Monday came and I was there early in the morning to pick him up at his house. I have a phone, but he didn't have a phone. Since he was part-time help, I was not going to buy a phone for him, because he was not responsible.

I knocked at his door and no one came to the door. I just shook my head, and knocked again, and went back to my truck. I turned the key, and at the same time, I looked up and the front door was opening and he was standing in his pajamas. I turned off the truck and he said, " Come in and sit on the couch." he would get dressed.

As I sat there looking out of his windows, the weather outside was not bad. The house that he lived in was all on one level. The house was a little small, the living room and kitchen were open to each other. The house was not very old. I went in the house and the couch was sitting on the south side of the wall of the living room and I sat down. There were three bedrooms, living room, kitchen, and a bathroom down the hall, off the kitchen was a utilities room.

And I turned my head and was looking out of the window to the north, I saw a wave moving slowly across the wall and it bent the windows that I was looking out.

This is how I saw it, but the glass didn't break in two, Then it was moving through the cabinets, items on the shelves stayed in place and didn't fall off or move at all, and on through the kitchen. I never would have ever seen it, if it was not for the windows bowing. After the windows there was a fish tank, and it did the same thing.

The wave moved on to the refrigerator, kitchen cabinets, and the sink and through the utilities room, and they all bent and warped. Then it was gone. If it wasn't for the items bending, I would have never have seen it moving, because it was clear.

It warped the things that it passed through, but it did not break them. No water fell out of the fish tank. No canned goods fell from where they were on the wall. It didn't hurt the refrigerator at all. Even the cabinets warped.

I said something to him about what was going through his house; "Did you see it pass through the bathroom?" he said, "No." Even the cabinets warped.

You would think that every item was made out of rubber. Just as it passed through items, they want back to normal. I don't know what it was, I don't even know why I saw it, but it was there, and that's all I can say. Maybe a tear in fabric or a warp in space and time? Maybe someone else has the answers? I only saw it moving.

Could this be the way that God was showing me there was more to life then what we actually see?

Little Old Man

When I first married Melanie, we went to the First Church of God on Alhambra Street, in Frankfort, Indiana. It was getting harder for the older Christians to climb up and down the steps. One day the pastor and the people took a vote to see how many would like to build a new church. Everyone was for it.

We built a new church and changed the name to Kelley Crossing Church of God, on Kelley Road, in Frankfort. As time moved on, our Pastor George had some health problems, and it was time to find a replacement.

So they formed a committee to reach out and see if a young pastor would come to Frankfort. They would hold interviews, and in time they found one. He was young and married, just out of college with no children yet.

They brought the vote to the front of the congregation, and called to see if he could come and see our church and give a little sermon. In the end we voted for Daniel Miller as God's leader for our church.

As time moved on, their lives were changing, they were having children, and at the same time the church was changing, too.

We were a church with a large sanctuary up in front of the congregation. We had a place for our baby grand piano, the organ, and place for the pulpit. There was a Remembrance Table down in front of the stage by the pulpit. At the back of the sanctuary, hanging on the wall was a cross.

Over time, the lights that were there when the new building was built were removed and replaced with spotlights. Now there are only two hanging lights. There were two cameras hanging from the ceiling, one for the left wall, one for the right wall. No more singing from the hymnals, the songs are being flashed upon the walls, with the words for the new song and used mostly for songs not found in the hymnals.

At the same time I had a dream. I saw an old man on his knees with some tools, working on something on the ground. You would think it was night time, because everything was in the dark. And it was hard to make out what some of the objects were.

Then he stood up and looked around, and picked up his tools. He headed back home for the night. He was tired and it was time to go home, to have his evening meal. The next morning it was another dark day. He was back working hard on his knees. I looked closer and saw that it was a foundation that he was patching. He would fix it during the day, and when he would go home, and come back in the morning, it had deteriorated more. No matter how fast he worked, it would be worse the next morning.

There was a dark cloud that moved over our church, and there was a change coming. Now the church would have a totally new look, and the church would go into a new birth. The old foundation of the church was falling apart, and the old man was the older people, who liked the church the way it was, before Pastor Daniel started changing things.

And when the old man looked to his left, he saw a Golden light, shining down on the flowering bush, which was sitting off on the outside corner of the foundation. There was a little bird going to every bloom on the plant.

This meant that there were younger people taking over the leadership operation of the church. Older people now had zero say in the church anymore; just keep putting your tithes in the offering plate. They wanted our ten percent, but not our knowledge.

After the pastor had his way and things were going well and I was doing some work in the church, he came up to me and said that everything was in its place and the sound system was working well.

I said, "When the day comes, and you decide to leave us, then what?" He had no comment. We were stuck with the new system. We paid for it, and it was now our responsibility. He would be somewhere else, with another church.

Within two years, he left for another ministry job, and now the job for us was to find a new person to fill the pulpit.

In our church, we were losing a lot of souls, through old age, some too sick to make it to church, some with Alzheimer's, some going into nursing homes, not able to live by themselves, not able to take their medicine or forget to keep up, lose time and what day it was.

In the end we did get a new pastor for our church, and he was working all the time with our pastor Daniel, our new pastor's name was Terrance Chatman. He also stayed about two years and then moved on. Our church is currently looking for new pastoral leadership.

Ten Dolls

When my electronics business was going under, it was because the products that we repaired were getting too reliable. We found that we were not able to pay our bills, and make a living from the repairs, so we closed the business for good.

I started another business at an indoor tennis club! And before that I started doing work for Color Tile, out of one business into another.

I was able to start working for Color Tile, installing floors for them. We moved from First Street to a bigger house over on Clay Street, in Frankfort, Indiana. My widowed mother-in-law would be moving in with us. She lived in Chicago, in the house that Melanie lived in as she was growing up. We needed a larger house to put our furniture in and have room for hers.

I was able to start working for Color Tile, installing floors for them. I put ceramic floors down at our new house, and I showed those pictures of my work. I would buy all of my material from Color Tile, and the manager of Color Tile saw an opportunity to have a new installer come and work for them.

My brother, Joe, was working for Carpetland USA, in Lafayette, Indiana. My work for Color Tile lasted for two years and they closed their doors. They went out of business.

I now was working for Carpetland as an installer. I had all the tools and a wet saw to cut the tile, all I needed was a job.

I received a work order from Carpetland to install ceramic tile in a kitchen and the foyer floor. As it turned out it was a small job. They wanted to make sure I knew how to do the work right and the customer was happy with the work. The job was in the south end of Lafayette, and the work would take two days to complete. It was summertime, and I was able to set my wet ceramic saw up in the front of the garage door. This way I could go from the kitchen, to the foyer, front door and moved back to the kitchen, operating from the garage and into the kitchen, and finish up in the garage. As I went in and out of the garage, I noticed a lot of boxes stacked against the back wall.

After many trips, in and out of the garage and kitchen, I was able to see that they were dolls in their original boxes. When they were purchased from the store, and shipped to the house.

The last day I worked on the floor, I was putting the grout in the cracks of the tile, as I was finishing up with the job. The owner pulled up in the driveway. He got out of his car, and he was looking the floor over and said it really looks good. He was very pleased with the way it turned out, and it enhanced the look of the floor and the foyer.

I pointed my finger at the dolls stacked against the back wall of the garage. I said, "I noticed that you had a lot of boxes with dolls in your garage, not the best place to store them."

He said, "I don't care, they were my ex-wife's. I am going to put them to the curb, and I don't care what happens to them."

I said, "We have girls in our church that would be happy to have them. Would you care if I take them and give them to them?"

He said, "Load them up in your truck and get them out of my garage, I'm tired of looking at them!"

"You will make some girls very happy, thank you." As I loaded them up, I counted to see how many there were, the total was ten dolls in ten boxes. As I drove down the road, I was wondering how many girls we had in our church.

When I arrived home, I told my wife Melanie that I had picked up ten dolls from one of my customers, to give to the girls in our church. I unloaded them from my truck, and I brought them into the house to let her see them.

On Sunday after services were over, we carried all the dolls into the church and laid them on the tables, and the girls came out to pick one that they liked. As it turned out, there were ten girls for the ten dolls. Of the ten girls, only one came back to say thanks for the doll. She was the pastor's daughter, Vila.

Sometimes in life, we come across a place in our life that the Bible has a story that plays out in our time, like when the lepers called to Jesus to heal them of their sickness. "Have pity on us," they said. Jesus told them to go and show themselves to the priests. And they were all healed from their leprosy. Later on, one did come back to say thanks, and Jesus said to him, "Were there not ten, but yet only one came back to say thanks."

Talking to Pastor Daniel

I was telling our new pastor about what happened to me on February 7, 2007. So I set up an appointment to come to his office, and talk to him about me being lifted up, and seeing the Lord. The day came for me to go to the church and see the pastor.

I pulled into the parking lot, and I saw the pastor's car there. It was on a Thursday, and the cleaning lady was working in the church, the same one in the pamphlet. After I parked my truck, I walked up to the door and just as I was about to touch the door, a voice in my head said, "He won't believe you."

I went into the office and proceeded to tell him about when I was lifted up and saw the Lord in all his glory. I told him how it all started, when I was waiting for some furniture to be delivered to our house, I was reading a book written by Edgar Cayce, *Christ and His Church*. How one person can make a difference, and I said to myself, "I'm going to be that one person. I'm not going to be in the world, but out of the world." Just at that time my heart jumped with joy, and I knew that the Lord was pleased with me.

I told him some other things, and he said he had to leave, so we got up. Pastor Daniel said that he never had any dreams. I said, "When you go to bed tonight, just ask the Lord to help you remember your dreams."

I saw him in the food market about week later, and he said that he did have a dream, but he didn't understand it. I said for him to tell me what the dream was about. He said, "I was standing at my front door, and there were a lot of men running around my house. They had Hazmat suits on. The Hazmat teams were in my attic, in the house, in the sewers outside. After Pastor Daniel told me about his dream, he said to me, "Do you know what that means?"

I said, "I think I do."

The hazmat men wore green suits. They were there to help you clean up your house: inside and outside. Your house is your flesh. Your mind first, then your body, then the people you meet, must be cleaned up before you can be lifted up to see the Lord.

UFOs

We were going to Anderson, Indiana. The date was December 25, 1999. It was Christmas Day. Amanda was up very early, to open up her Christmas gifts, so we sent her down to see if Santa Claus had come during the night.

The next thing we knew she was back with her eyes full of excitement, pulling on us to get up, and go make sure Grandma, (Melanie's mother), was awake. Then we all were headed downstairs to sit in front of the Christmas tree, and Amanda wanted to pass out the gifts to everyone.

By the time we loaded the car up with gifts for the afternoon party, at Anderson Indiana, it was a little after twelve o'clock. I was driving down State Road 28, going east. It was a sunny day, but the sky was covered with a heavy haze in the sky.

I looked over to see how everyone was doing. They had gone to sleep. I looked out my car window and up into the sky. There was a stripe of haze that was gone as far north as you could see, something had cut the haze out of the sky, and it was clear blue, as if someone took a knife to it, and removed a piece, out of the haze in the sky.

I was trying to keep looking to see what it was. Then coming up the middle was a jet fighter chasing something, but all I could see was the jet. It was half the width of the space of the haze that was cut out.

The open blue space and the jet were heading due north. I watched it for two minutes and the jet veered to the right like it was headed to Fort Grissom Air Force Base.

At this time the others were still sleeping on, when we got to State Road 9. I turned right onto the highway. Now I was headed south to Anderson, Indiana.

If Only I Had a Stick

I was in Bob Byrd's office one day. I was checking on the insurance for my TV repair business.

I don't know how we got on the subject, but I was telling him something that happened, about me and God. It was when my work van got stuck in the snow on a lonely road. The only one that was around to help was the Lord.

Bob said, "Let me tell you what happened to me, one day around Halloween. I had an appointment, up north of Reynolds, Indiana, at a farmer's house, just south of Monon, Indiana.

To get to the farmer's house, I traveled on State Road 43 north. He said he was just south of Reynolds. It would be the first thing you see as you enter into the town, from the south end."

There is a church with a large statue of Christ standing on a pedestal. Christ has raised both arms up in the air, as if to say, "All may come." But someone had put a pumpkin on each hand. This bothered Bob, but he couldn't stop then. He was running late to his appointment with the farmer.

He told him what he had seen, coming into the town of Reynolds. The farmer only laughed and didn't think anything about it, but it upset Bob. He made a mental point to stop by the church and find help to get the pumpkins down.

After finishing with the farmer, he said that he headed back on State Road 43 south to Reynolds.

He pulled into the parking lot. To see if he could get some help, but he couldn't see any cars or people around. He knocked on the door, but no one answered.

So he went back to see if he could get the pumpkins off by himself, but the statue was too high up. He looked around to see if there was something he could use to get the pumpkins down. A stick would work, if there only was one on the ground, but there were only evergreen trees around. The statue was standing alone out in the open.

What Bob said about the church and the town is true; I've been through the town many times, going on service calls. At that time I was in the TV repair business.

So after looking at the statue, and feeling hopeless, he thought to himself, "If only I had a stick." No sooner where the words out of his mouth than he heard a loud thud behind him. He turned to look and there on the ground was a stick. He picked it up and it was just long enough to reach the pumpkins. He had freed Christ's hands.

When he drove back to Lafayette, Indiana, he had a warm feeling, because it felt good to know that he was not alone, and he did the right thing.

This story was told to me by Robert Byrd, in his office around the 1980s.

Working in Chicago

Gil called to let me know that he had a job for me. I would be working for Jack Daniels. Jack is a black man and he lives in the heart of Chicago. I didn't mind. He gave me the phone number. "Call him up," said Gil. I said, "OK. I'll call him and we can talk about what he wants me to work on."

He wanted a major overhaul in his bathroom on the first floor. I got the address and a time to meet him. "Monday morning," he said, "come around 8:30 a.m. and I'll be home."

I was up early so I would have enough time to get to his home. I found his house and he said to come to the side door of the house. It had bars all around the house windows, and the doors. He came to the side door and let me in.

He said, "Come on in." He showed me the bathroom. I looked it over. He wanted all new wiring, all the walls torn out, and the bathtub, and a new whirlpool tub in its place.

He said, "Can you do it?"

I said, "Yes, but how are you going to pay for it, and all the other materials?"

Jack said, "With cash. Let's get in my car and go to Menard's and order what we need."

I asked Jack, "Where do you work?"

He said, "For Jack Daniels."

"Do you mean the one that makes the whiskeys?"

"Yes!" Jack said.

"Do you spell your name the same way he does?"

"Yes, I do," said Jack.

"I go to different taverns and buy drinks for the customer in the tavern."

I said, "Do you get drunk every night?"

"No, I tell the bar tender to serve me only Cokes, not whiskeys, the truth is I don't drink at all."

We went inside and ordered everything I told him I needed. Jack paid with cash. As we were heading back to his house, he said he had a friend who would like me to look at his front room and see if I could sand it and put a finish on it.

I said, "What's his name?"

"Winston."

As it turned out, Winston was black also, but very friendly. I looked at the floor and told him I could do it tomorrow. I would need to wait until Jack's materials would come in. I said to Winston, "Do you have a credit card? We need to rent a buffer to sand the floor and get sandpaper for the unit. "I don't have any credit cards, is it ok if we use your credit card to pick-up what we need?"

"The only thing your need to pay me for is the labor."

"Ok!" He said.

"I'll be back tomorrow, around nine o'clock. When I arrived at Winston's house, I knocked on the door." His wife came to the door. I told her why I was there and then, Winston came from the back room. "Let's go and get what we need over at Home Depot."

When we got back to his house, I started working on the floor. Winston had everything in the room moved out. His wife came into the room I was working in, and asked me my name. I told her "Bill," and I went back to work, about an hour later she came by and asked me my name, I said, "Bill."

About two hours later, I was done with sanding the floor and was getting ready to put the finish on the floor, when his wife came by and wanted to know what my name was.

"Bill," I said.

I told Winston not to let his wife step on the floor, after I put the first coat on.

It wasn't long before I was back up at Winston's home, and his wife said, "Who are you?"

"Bill," I said, then I went to work putting the last coat of finish on the floor.

I talked to Winston and said something about his wife not remembering me. He knew she had a problem. When he couldn't be home he would take her to his church. The women there would take care of her until he came back to pick her up. Most of her life, she was a nurse.

He paid me and said to me, "Here's the bill for the buffer and the sandpaper. They didn't charge us for the sand paper, just the buffer." The cost for the sandpaper came to $20. I was running late, I thought to myself that I'll pay Home Depot when I come and work on Jack's bathroom.

In a couple of days, Jack called me up to tell me that he had picked up all the material at Menard's, "I'll get started on Monday and with any luck, I should be done by Friday."

I arrived at his home early Monday Morning, and knocked on the door.

Jack came to let me in. I saw he had everything in the dining room. "Come in and set down with me at the kitchen table."

"What would you charge me to do the dining room and the kitchen floor? Gil has some tile that I can buy at a good price."

"I would say one thousand dollars for labor. It should take me a week to do."

I worked on the bathroom, tearing out the bathtub and putting it on a carpet to slide it on the floor and down the step to the side door, where I had a hand truck waiting. I rolled it out to the alley, and set the tub out of the way so a car could get in and out of the alley. I had some piping that I needed take out to the alley next. When I stepped in the alley a minute later, the tub that was made of cast iron was gone. No one in sight; the tub was gone!

I started putting in new wiring, and water lines. As I worked day after day, I would hear noise coming from the basement. But when I would go down there, and started working on the electrical wiring and the water lines, there was no one down there. When I would go up to the bathroom, then the noise would start. It sounded like someone was moving objects and putting them up.

I didn't always see Jack every day. Jack gave me a key to get in from the side door. On that day when I was finishing up on the bathroom, he was sitting at the kitchen table. He motioned for me to set down.

"Well Jack, how does the bathroom look to you?"

"Really good, and here's the money for the bath and here's the money for the tile that you will be starting Monday."

"I should have everything done in the bath by one o'clock, then you can pay me, and I'll be coming back at the first of next week." He was reaching into his pocket, and pulled out the money for the floor and put it on the kitchen table.

"Here is the money for the dining room and kitchen," Jack said. "I might not be in town next week. I trust that you will do the job." "Give it to your wife. When I'm done, she can pay me then."

On the way home from Jack's house, as I was nearing Lafayette, just north of State Road 43, the clouds were puffy, but they had round holes punched out of them. And as I headed around Lafayette, on the east side of the road, there were more holes punched in the clouds, about the size of a two car garage, and also smaller ones, the size of a single car garage. All in all there were a dozen holes. I only saw them around Lafayette; I drove on south on Interstate 65 south, to State Road 28 east, to Frankfort.

And I still think about those holes in the clouds. A lot of times, people don't always talk about the things that are unusual, that happen in their life.

I was up early Monday morning; before the sun was up, carrying out the trash to the alley. As I was walking back along my garage to come into the house and get my coffee, there was a shiny object coming out of the west heading east, not moving very fast. As it got closer to me, this is what I noticed about it.

It was shaped like a cigar, metallic in color, made no sound, had no markings or windows on it. Its speed was about thirty-five miles an hour. When I held my hand and arm up to get its size, it measured from my finger tips to my elbow. I ran around the garage to the alley to get the last look as it went out of sight behind the trees. I had a feeling it was one of ours. I thought to myself, "That is one of ours."

I picked up my coffee and had all my tools that I needed for the floor, and headed to I-65 north to Chicago, and Jack's house. It took me a week to do the work, and the noise in the basement was always there. No one else ever heard it, but me. I was the only one that could hear it in the basement moving around.

When I finished the job, Jack's wife was there to pay me.

"How would you like to do the other bathroom up on the second floor?"

"I can't, I have another job in Lafayette that will take up a lot of my time. But I can see if Chuck can do it for you, I'll have him call you."

When I Was Lifted Up

It was February 7, 2007, a lot like all other mornings, as I left the house and headed out of Frankfort, on Indiana State Road 28 west. It was a clear day. The sun was shining and the temperature was around thirty-five to forty degrees.

Lafayette was about thirty minutes away on State Road 52 north. But unlike any ordinary day, this would be one to remember for the rest of my life.

I drove into RPM (restoring property management). This was a company that I worked for which rented apartments for the owners and collected the monthly rent. I needed to get a check after I clocked in. Then I had to go down Union Street to Bell Parts to pick up the order for one of the apartments.

I left RPM a little past 8:00 a.m. and turned onto Earl Avenue. I stopped at the light at the intersection of Union and Earl. Then I turned left, going west on Union to Twenty-First Street, where Union become a one-way street, and Salem Street turns into a one-way street going west.

I maneuvered into the left lane to make the turn at Ninth Street. I had gotten as far as Eighteenth Street and Salem when something unexplained occurred.

There was a car in front of me, and as I approached the light, it was green, but suddenly turned yellow. My foot went to the brake pedal of my old, red Dodge Ram truck, and I noticed an object on the outside of the window on the right passenger's side of the vehicle.

This is where I first saw the sphere on the outside of ᵣ TRUCK

Rear view of my truck from the inside.

It was in the form of a sphere, clear in the center, with a brown rim around it. As I pressed the break harder and came to a stop, it moved over toward me. When I came to a full stop, it was directly in front of me.

As I peered at it, for a second, to better see what it could be, I realized I was no longer in the truck, but was standing on a wall. An angel with a dark brown robe was standing next to me there. I assumed he had been the one who had transported my soul out of my body and away from my truck. Now I understood that he had been the sphere outside my windshield.

As I stood there, on the step of the wall, everything I saw was bright white, but it didn't hurt my eyes. I could see very clearly that there was a path between me and the distant wall, which had seven steps. It was also a brilliant white, and beyond the wall was a glowing haze. I could see an arch in the landscape. There was no sun, just light, and a hazelike fog as my eyes followed the steps to my right, everything I viewed was a luminous glow.

As my eyes came back down the path, I noticed that there was an object in the middle of the path, which was much brighter than the path itself. I followed it with my eyes, and realized it was the back of a person standing there. All could see was a garment with a ten-foot train coming from the back of the person's robe.

At this very moment I felt my whole body flooded with the very essence of love unlike any I had ever known before! Then instantly, I was back in the truck, the tears of joy coming down my cheeks. I cried out, "Oh, no, Lord," as the light turned green. I headed toward Bell Parts with my mind deep in thought.

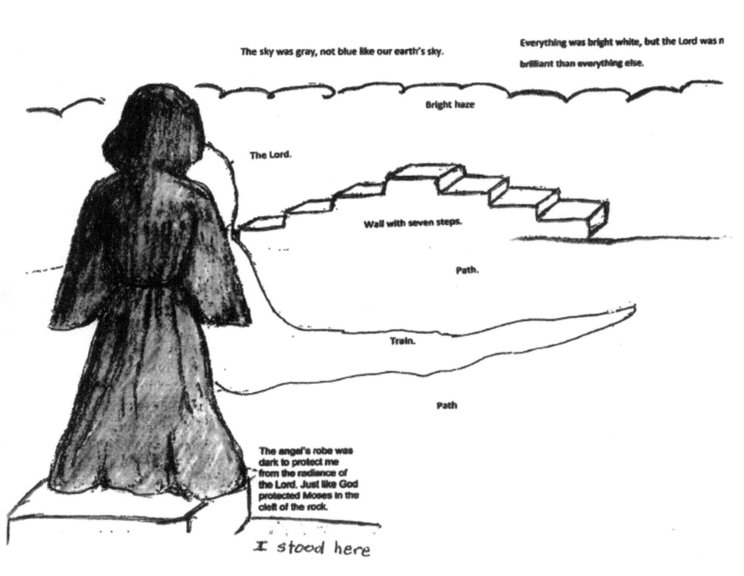

The sky was gray, not blue like our earth's sky.

Everything was bright white, but the Lord was n
brilliant than everything else.

Bright haze

The Lord.

Wall with seven steps.

Path.

Train.

Path

The angel's robe was dark to protect me from the radiance of the Lord. Just like God protected Moses in the cleft of the rock.

I stood here

For months after this experience, I could feel a glowing tingle inside my flesh, like the outline of another body inside of me—like my soul.

Many people at church, never knew that they were receiving a little of that light, some of the glow from the Lord, when I would shake their hands. I didn't tell some of the people, but I did tell my pastors at the church. There was no response from them.

After that, I kept my experience with the Lord to myself for a long time. However, the Lord spoke to me in a dream, and told me I needed to tell God's children what he did for me, that he was still working in the world today.

So I told everyone in my Sunday school class, but seemingly to no avail. There was only one person in the church who asked me to tell what I had been talking about, because she had only heard the very end.

So I told her, our church cleaning woman. The only one who took interest in my witness? How Biblical is that? The story didn't end here.

Two years later, on April 9, 2009, I was home waiting for some new furniture to be delivered. I was reading a book called Edgar Cayce's *Story of Jesus*, and on page 29 it talks about John 8:56–58. It said, "Your father rejoiced to see my day, and he saw it and was glad. Then the Jews said to him, you are not yet fifty years old, and have you seen Abraham? Jesus said to them, most assuredly, I say to you, before Abraham was, I AM."

If you look up Genesis chapter 14, verse 18, it reads: "Then Melchizedek King of Salem brought out bread and wine, he was the priest of God Most High." You may think to yourself, "So what?" But for me, there it was: confirmation in the Bible that my experience was truly from the Lord. You see, my vision occurred at the intersection of Eighteenth and Salem!

This was the Lord's way of showing the doubters who only believe in the written scriptures that what I saw was real. I stood with the Lord on the distant wall! And He is still working in the world.

The Lord's Joy and Love

The joy of the Lord is upon me
The joy of His love has touched me
He has lifted me up and placed me on seven steps
He has let me see His Glory
He has let me feel His Love
He floods my soul with His overwhelming Love
This Joy and Love I carry with me
In my heart and my soul
What a Joy it is to have found that Love
It will never leave me. It has taken hold of me
Now it feeds my soul.

Seeing the Mother of Christ

When I was lifted up and saw the Lord, I asked Him who it was, that called my name on that summer evening when I was coming home from work. When I was walking down the driveway to the Cary Home, about half way, a woman called my name two times.

That night I went to bed, and in a dream I was standing in a clearing, in the center of the woods. All around me were trees. There was a small hill in front of me with some trees growing up the hillside.

I heard some noise coming from in front of me, which sounded like running water. When I looked down I saw a bubbling brook of water in front of me. The water was dancing with bubbles, jumping up and down.

When I looked up, I saw Mary step out from behind a tree. That was on the side of the hill. Her hood was white and the robe was all blue. And then I looked at her face. I have never see any one with that much beauty.

She spoke to me in my mind.

"Would you like to cross the stream?"

I said, "No, my work here is not yet done." If I would have crossed the stream to the other side, I would have been stuck on the other side. But I had work to do. The main reason was that I was starting to write a book about my life, from birth to now.

Then she was gone, I opened my eyes. I now know who it was that spoke to me over fifty-two years later, as I walked down the driveway to the Cary Home, and why the water was so happy. Mary was coming and the bubbles in the brook knew it.

I don't know what would have happened if I would have stepped across the water to the other side. This book wouldn't have been written. This is the way I look at the outcome. This is why my work wasn't done; I still had a book to write on the material side of earth.

My work was to tell others how the Lord had lifted me up and told me to tell His children, and what He did for me. When people buy the book, they will read what happened to me as I traveled through this life.

Mary

Beginning and End

Telling God's Children What He Did for Me

This dream happened two years after I was lifted up and saw the Lord.

The sky was blue, the day was starting off as a great day, and the weather was warm. I was standing on a green grassy node, in front of an adobe house that was a light brown. There was an opening for a door, and two openings for windows, but no door or windows on the adobe house.

I heard a radio voice coming out of the adobe house. It was saying that there was an all-out movement going on, all around the world, where they were picking up people who were talking and lifting up the love of God and the Lord. When they found them, they would put them in jail, put them where the people couldn't hear them or see them. They were trying to smash the word of God.

As I stood there, to my right, I was looking at a large hill of snow, fifty feet wide by one hundred fifty feet long, ten feet tall. I was thinking that it was odd, that I was looking at a pile of snow in the summertime. It should have melted in this warm weather.

I was trying to understand what the snow meant. Up in the far left corner, there was a long black car coming down the the side road. It came to the end of the road, and it made a left turn toward me.

I started moving toward the pile of snow. As I entered into the snow. It was more like a thick fog than snow. I could see through the fog, and see them coming my way in their car. Two men got out of the vehicle. They stopped where I just entered into the snow. Everything about their dress attire was black, they wore hats, and even the car was black. By this time I could hear the car doors shut.

Then one of them said, "Didn't he just walk into that pile of snow?"

The other one said, "Yes he did, let's go and put him under arrest, and take him back to headquarters and book him in."

I could see them as they moved by me, but they didn't see me standing there. Then one of them said, "Let's go back to headquarters and bring more men to help find him."

As they were leaving I came out of the snow, and walked to the top of the hill, and I looked up and here they were coming down the road again, now there were two vehicles that were black. They made a left hand turn toward me in their vehicles.

I walked down the hill and into the white snow, and it wasn't long before they were walking by me. I could see them, but they couldn't see me.

After walking all over but not able to find me, the one that was in charge said, "Let's go and get a truck load of men. I know he is in here; I saw him walk in. We just need more help." They walked out and got into the cars and left.

I came out to the top of the hill, and when I looked up, there they were coming in two cars, and a half ton truck, full of men, dressed in black. I started walking toward the snow, and the next thing I knew there were three children around me, saying, "Don't go, we want you to stay with us." Then I woke up from the dream.

This is what the dream means to me. The brown adobe house represents the simple life. The pile of snow, is the spirit of the Lord in the world that we live in.

There is a greater greed to have a need for everything that man has manufactured, which will make our lives easier and more fun. When you live in large cities the only thing you see is what man creates, not what God created, and people get lost and lose sight of God.

Wherever you look, how many people go from pay check to pay check, from week to week, just dreaming that they would hit the big lottery? And they wouldn't have the worldly problems; they would be sitting on easy street. What a life! Then the dream goes up in a puff of smoke. And then it's time to go back to work.

This is how the masses are controlled: keep them entertained, under habits that they can enjoy, even when they grow old. This life in not about how much you can get from this world, but how much love you can put in it. All in all, you will have a much richer life as a person, when you enter the Kingdom.

There was a man who won the lottery. Now he was very rich, but he didn't believe in banks. He hid all his money in his house. The story could end there, and we could say that the house burned down to the ground. But that's not the way it ends. His last will and testament was for his wife to put all his money in his casket when he would pass away and die. He said he was going to take it with him, and told her to promise to do what his wishes were.

As time went on he would tell her to do what he wanted her to do again. He would make her promise to do his will. And she said, "I will, dear."

Then the day came, he was dying. He called her into his bedroom, where he kept his money in his mattress: a million dollars! He was a happy man. He would be the first man to take his money to his grave. Two days later, his life was about over for him.

He passed away, and his wife was standing next to the casket. She had kept her promise to her husband. As the lid was being closed, she dropped a check that was worth a million dollars into his casket. Bottom line is; you just can't take it with you.

By loving other people and helping them to find God in their lives, you are putting your worth in God's bank. Now you will be getting a better return on your love.

Nativity Scene

This dream is about a small town in Frankfort, Indiana, the courthouse and business around the square.

The time is night. No one is downtown, just me. The first thing I noticed was that everything was dark. The streetlights were off. The stores had lights, but they were very faint, not shining on the sidewalks, but only inside of the stores.

At the corner of Main and Clinton, I heard music coming out of a speaker, that was hooked low on a lamp pole, playing "Peace on Earth." When I looked up from the speaker, I was facing the courthouse.

There were no lights on the courthouse, or in the courthouse. But on the outer edge of the curb, were standing ten foot panels of stained glass. The first scene was of angels up in the sky on a starry night, and shepherds in the fields, that were keeping watch over their sheep at night. The angels were telling of the birth of the Christ Child that was being born.

The heavenly host were singing "Peace on Earth". And in the background, evergreen trees standing behind the panels to the left and the far right corner. There were lights coming from behind the glass, that were on the inside of the panels, that lit it up so you could see all the colors coming through.

As I moved, I was walking east on Clinton Street. The music would change as I walked to the far end of the scene. There was another scene of the Christ child. In a cave stood Mother Mary and Joseph, looking down at the child, and over them a star shining down on the Child.

At the ends of the four corners, there are four fifteen-foot cathedral openings, where you can enter into the inside and go into the courthouse. This was made with multi colors of glass with lead cane to hold the glass in place.

Going north on Jackson Street, there were houses, and the scene changed to a winter scene. People were standing in their winter coats holding candles in in their hands, in front of the homes singing songs. As I moved along the sidewalk, in front of the scenes, and the scene would change, so did the songs.

When I left Jackson Street, I turned onto Washington Street, there wasn't a scene. That end was open for suggestion from the people that would turn in their suggestion of what the scene would be on that end of the street.

When I turned on Main Street, from one end to the other end, there was a full size sled with Santa and his reindeer flying over the roof tops of houses. And Rudolph led the team with his glowing red nose. The moon was bright and full.

The music was playing softly, "Santa Claus is Coming to Town.". The music was clear and sharp.

There were so many people coming to see the scene, they had to park them outside of the town and bus them in. They were coming from everywhere and from out of the country.

This was the most outstanding Christmas display ever put on by a small town. There was news coverage from all over the world.

The airport was busy, with planes coming and going.

The panels could be broken down into ten-foot setions. The parts that held it up, are the doors for the panels, that closed up the stain glass to protect the scenes, when moving it away or storing it away in a barn for safe keeping.

The sections were on low riding wheels that kept the unit low to the ground, when moving the scenes from the barn to the courthouse. The lights that were used were not spotlights, but a soft light.

The Night I Saw My Soul

One of the things I noticed was that when I was out of my body, I never saw my soul. The first time this happened, was when I was staying at the Thayer's, after I was discharged from the army.

It was summertime. We didn't have an air conditioner to cool the house down. In August it would get very hot and humid in the evening. I left my bedroom early in the morning and went to the front living room. I was trying to cool off and get some sleep on the couch.

After I fell to sleep, I found myself sitting up and looking around, and there was a light that filled the rooms. It had a golden haze to it. I was looking out into the kitchen. I could see the stove, front door, and refrigerator next to the table and a window.

I turned and looked down and saw myself sleeping on the couch, and then my soul entered and lay back down on my flesh. I opened my eyes and I rose up with my body. I was now looking with my flesh eyes into the kitchen, I couldn't see anything, and it was completely dark in the room.

When I was lifted up, and my soul was standing next to an angel, I didn't see my soul then. This started the whole thing about my soul. That was when I asked, "Why don't I ever see my soul?"

It started out with me going to bed. I would be seeing how my soul works with my body. I find it very hard to explain how the soul works with the body, they are two beings, and when separated they become two: one flesh, the other one spirit. They operate independently of one another, and know what one or the other is seeing or hearing. This is the best I can explain it.

I crawled into bed and pulled the covers up to my chin, and as I lay there getting ready to go to sleep, I noticed that I could see my eye lids close and open, I was looking at my eyelids from the inside of my soul eyes. I was seeing the back of the eye lids from the inside of my flesh, as they were blinking. The difference was I was looking with my soul eyes, that were inside of my body. It was not the flesh or my earthly eyes that I was looking through. It was through my soul eyes.

Then I was back, looking from my flesh eyes, and watching my spirit leave my fleshly body. The spirit floated to the end of my bed and stopped and stood a little to the right of my feet. The next thing I saw was my spirit looking at me. I was now looking at my body lying in bed, through the soul eyes; I could see the covers were pulled up to my neck.

Then I was back in my flesh, looking at my spirit. The glow of the spirit, was white in color. It didn't light up the room, but stayed with the spirit.

I could see that the spirit was made up of a head, main body, arms, and legs. There was no hair on its head. You could see what was standing behind it. In this case, it was a dresser and the wall.

I could see objects, from the head down to the mid-section, seven in all, they must be spiritual centers. They were showing how advanced the spirit was in its spiritual climb. As I lay there I could feel what the spirit felt, a blissful and joyous feeling over the whole body.

Then it started moving back toward the flesh. Very slowly it entered into my body. I could feel heaviness as it touched my body, the flesh started pulling on the spirit, and it was locked in my body. The spirit was completely in the flesh. Now they were one soul.

I think about all the experiences that have happened to me. The Lord being the top one, then having my soul coming out of my body and being able to see it move from the flesh to the spirit, and knowing what I was seeing, being able to know what was going on in my body and spirit, coming together as one soul, at the same time.

The spirit and the body are one soul, when they are together. They are independent of each other, as long as the flesh is alive, or the spirit is removed by a greater force. As when I was lifted out of my body and found myself standing next to an angel on seven steps, and back in the truck, my flesh was in the truck holding the breaks on, until the light changed, not aware that I was out of my body.

Then I was put back in my flesh, and at that moment I saw the light change green, I headed for Bell Parts. Then the body saw and knew what I saw and felt.

Or when I was in hell, and my body was in bed, I still was able to communicate with my body, and tell it to open its eyes, so I could be free from hell.

Floating above the trees, then I came down to a path and moved along it, floating above the path. But still I was not able to see my soul. This was what led to this vision, of me seeing my soul.

This is the end of my time line, for now. It's been a long road from four years old to seventy-six years old. When my friends ask me how my health is, I just say, "Better than you will ever know."

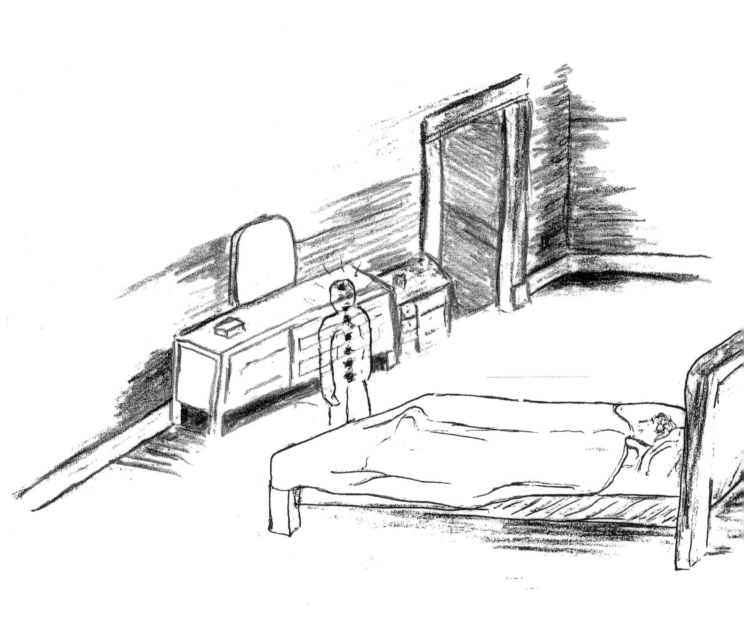

The Night I saw My Soul

Path

The very last dream I had was a picture of a path coming out of the woods, with trees on the right side and on the left side. The trees look like trees of paradise.

Then there was a path that was running from the center of the trees and going out into a meadow that went on out to the horizon. With the path in the middle, there was an arched sign that was floating in the air, with words on it that said, "God's Love for Us All."

Last Picture of the Path

The last picture I saw in my dream was the one of the path with a sign hanging in the sky that reads, "God's Love for Us All."

There were two trees growing at the edge of paradise, where God lives, representing the beginning of new life for us.

At the end of the path is where God waits for his children to come home.

The archway, hanging like a rainbow in the sky, stands for God's promise to us that he would not destroy the earth by flood, and is a covenant between us.

Once we go down the believer's path to our heavenly home, we are home forever.

All believers are welcome to come enter the arch of God's forgiveness, protection, and love.

Precognition

Is there a time when the Lord stops needing your help? I'm now seventy-eight years old, and the Lord has shown me that He still will use me when needed.

There were two events that happened to me in March 2019; the first one was on a Sunday as my wife and I were just leaving Kelley Crossing Church of God. We decided to eat at The Great Wall of China restaurant, in our hometown of Frankfort, Indiana.

As I was getting my food, I saw a tall black man. I walked up to him and said, "I know you, and I've seen you before, in my dreams." Then I showed him the pamphlet and explained what happened to me on February 7, 2007. He took the pamphlet and went back to his table. I returned to my table and told my wife what just had happened to me. I saw all of this happen before at an earlier time, in real time. This means that God has events already set up in my life that I still need to do.

On March 24–28, 2019, members of my family went to Tennessee for vacation: my wife Melanie, our daughter Amanda, her husband Allen, and their children Owen, Adilynn, Ryne, and Russell. Also accompanying us were Allen's parents John and Deb Marciniak. On our way back home, we decided to stop and eat at a Frisch's Big Boy restaurant.

We needed placement for eight people; we were shown a table in the back where there was enough room for that many people. Then we were all seated and the menus passed out and our drink orders were taken.

As I sat there looking around, I saw that there was another table that was not being used. About at that time, I saw a waitress bring a group in to sit at that table. As they entered, I recognized them from a dream before. When they were seated, I went over to their table and gave them one of my pamphlets and told them I had seen them before. As I was talking to the woman who came in last and explained my experience, one of the men said that she was the pastor of their church.

These two events are showing me that God is still sending me people to share my vision of His love. Old age is not a limiting factor to God.

How Did This Man Know Who I Was

My wife (Melanie) and I were going to Cabo Mexico, our plane landed in Los Angeles airport, we departed from the plane and pick-up our luggage, to check in for San José del Cabo Mexico.

As I was told to go down to the last check through and I took out everything that was in my pockets, and put them in a tray, as my items were scanned, I was scanned also. I moved to the end of the table, put all my items back in my pockets and put my shoes back on.

With my shoes on, I looked up and there was a man staring at me, and another person behind the first man, I put my hands into my pocket to get a pamplet out, to show him what had happened to me on February 9th, 2007.

I pulled out my pamphlet and he said, "I know who you are William Holsclaw," then he turned and went down the hall and through two doors, then they were gone.

I told my wife what happened to me as I was being checked through the line. I didn't know who he was nor have I ever seen him before. I didn't know who he was, he was thin, he moved around like he was in charge of the place, but no one was paying any attention to them.

Real Time That Is Different

It was around 2:00 in the morning, I was moved to get out of bed, I needed to relieve my bladder. As I was sitting there in the dark, a light on the south side of the house, like I have never seen before, came through the two windows. The light was within itself, it didn't light up the whole room with light, and then it was gone. It was not real, it didn't reflect off of the floor, or anything else in the room. There was no noise like a plane, and it wasn't coming from the neighbors' house. Our house sits two levels higher than theirs by ten feet. If the light was coming from their house, it would be shining up, not down.

The date was January 28, 2020. The next thing I knew, I was standing in a room that was 12x12 feet, and the lights were very dim. I couldn't tell where it was coming from. The walls looked like they were made from metal, light gray in color. When I looked around, the room had nothing in it but three gray shapes. They were looking at me and one of them was talking to me in my mind, asking questions about seeing and standing in front of Christ. Then I told them about standing in front of the Lord, and that an angel had taken my spirit out of my flesh. Then I was back in my bedroom.

I went to sleep again. I was back in the same dimly lit room, and the three gray shapes couldn't understand how I was able to see and know about my soul. I told them that I have a spirit and a body, what one sees and hears, the other one sees and hears. If the flesh is between awake and asleep, it knows what's going on, and they both retain it as a memory. When the body goes to sleep, it doesn't know what the spirit is doing and where it goes, but when the flesh wakes up, the spirit is pulled back into the body, and stays in the body. The only way it can become free of the body is when the flesh dies, the spirit is free, but not to roam in the earth plane, but is pulled to another higher light and plane.

I don't think they understood what I was trying to tell them, because they didn't have a soul, and they found it hard to believe what I was trying to tell them. Then I was back in my bedroom.

Without a soul there is no life for the flesh, in the first man, GOD breathed life in man and woman, (which was a soul in the man and a soul in the woman.) As I was trying to think about what happened to me, why were they (the grays) confused? They were just machines, but able to think, very intelligent, but they didn't have souls and couldn't understand why I had a soul or that there was two of me.

I - 65 South

On Friday, July 31, 2020, I was going to pick-up my grand-son. Owen, at his home and take him to Indianapolis, for his boxing lesson, starting at 4:30 PM.

I was on I-65 south, when I came to I-865 bypass, that would take me east to State Road 421 going south to 86st Street.

As I was coming out of the turn on I-865 east, there was a semi in front me about a half mile in front me. My speed was 70 to 72 miles per hour. I was coming up on the semi truck. I looked into my rearview mirror to make sure there wasn't any vehicle coming up on my left side.

A half mile back, coming out of turn from I-65 S, I saw a van, tan in color. I had one of them for a work truck, 20 years ago. The one I used to drive, never moved that fast.

I moved over into the left lane, and at that time the van did too. I was coming upon another semi, and the van was getting closer to my car. I glanced up in front of me to see if I had room to get over and out of the way of van that was coming. The eighteen-wheeler had me blocked, so I was stuck in my lane.

I moved over into the left lane, and at that time the van did too. I was coming upon another semi, and the van was getting closer to my car. I glanced up in front of me to see if I had room to get over and out the way of van that was coming. The eighteen-wheeler had me blocked, so I was stuck in my lane.

When I looked in my rear view mirror, the truck was right on my bumper of the car. I tried to see who was driving the van, but it was dark inside. Darkness was the only thing I could see. When I checked the road in front of me, there was no where to go to get out of the way.

I kept checking my rear view mirror to see what was going on. The van was gone, the scene in the mirror was only blue sky, there was nothing behind me. Where did the van go?

I looked up to see where the semi was. It had turned to go up on the ramp, that was heading to I-465 S. how could the van have disappeared so fast? What was going on? Just another example of God protecting me.

Golden Gates of Heaven

In this dream, I found myself and my wife, (Melanie) walking arm and arm toward an open staircase. It started out like a football stadium, where you walk up to your seats, turn around and sit down to watch the game being played on the field below. However, this stadium was enclosed. You had to walk through a door and up some steps into a foyer. What made these steps different was that they were made of Gold. The steps, rails, and the floors were also made of gold. The lights we could see were like a golden haze, coming from the Golden Gates, at the very top.

We stopped, when we came to the entrance of the foyer, coming out of the hall. We looked up and saw that it was a very long way to the top of the Golden Gates. We started moving forward as we climbed up the steps. There were people sitting on the benches, to my right side and to my left, as far as I could see, all the way to the Golden Gates. The stadium seats were different, they didn't face downward, but faced up, just the reverse of what you'd expect, at a normal sports stadium. There were people from my family, which I knew. I thought to myself, "Why were they just sitting there? Why didn't they get up and go through the Golden Gates?"

All the people were leaning forward, as if to get a better look at the Golden Gates. They didn't see Melanie and me. They were staring straight ahead, like they were in a trance. As we moved to the top and stopped at the last step, I saw they were sitting on seats made of bright red cherry wood. The first row of people could have fallen through the Gates, that was how close they were to the entrance of the Golden Gates. Then it hit me what the problem was: they were held back by their earthly possessions, the material things of earth we work so hard to accumulate in our lifetime. The more we have the harder it is to give them up.

The souls will sit there until a New Light dawns on them, and unlocks them from their earthly possessions, positions in life, and their wealth.

Written by: William W. Holsclaw

The end.

I Took a Beating for you!

Wm. Holloan

About the Author

William Holsclaw was born on August 4, 1941, as the seventh child of a family of eventually nine. He was drafted in the army in December 1962 and served at Fort Knox, Kentucky, and later Fort Sill, Oklahoma. William found the love of his life when a picture of him was given to a fifth-grade teacher while he was given a picture of the teacher, Melanie Werner. They went on a blind date and continued dating for two years. They married on June 5, 1976, at the First Church of God in Oak Lawn, Illinois. Together they have a daughter, Amanda Kay, and four wonderful grandchildren: Owen, Adilynn, Ryne, and Russell. William has always enjoyed creative endeavors such as drawing, wood carving, furniture making, and colored glass projects such as lamps and windows. He is also an avid tennis player and has enjoyed both softball and bowling. William knows in his heart that God loves us and that we are never alone. It is his hope that his grandchildren will read his work and remember that they are never alone and that God loves them!

CPSIA information can be obtained
at www.ICGtesting.com
Printed in the USA
LVHW072033250421
685556LV00002B/6